METAVERSE

Daniel L. Bray

Page intentionally left blank

TABLE OF CONTENTS

INTRODUCTION

Following Facebook's rebranding as Meta, a fresh buzz arose around the term "Metaverse," but no one knew what it meant. For many years, there has been a lot of speculation about how the internet and technology would progress. When we talk about the evolutionary phases of the internet, we commonly refer to Web1, Web2, Web3, and so on, and now we're talking about the Metaverse.

But ignore the definitions for a moment and consider the following scenario: Imagine being able to build your ideal alter-ego in a virtual environment where you have complete power. You can do anything you want, possess whatever you want, and your options are nearly endless.

A scenario like this has been presented in many science fiction films and television shows. However, it may become a reality soon because there is a lot of buzz in the business world about getting every layer, technology, and protocol ready to develop "The Metaverse."

What is the Metaverse?

People can work, socialize, transact, play, and even create in the Metaverse, a highly scalable, permanent network of interconnected virtual worlds centered on real-time interaction. It immerses the user in the virtual world using advanced virtualization and technologies (AR,

VR, Haptic Sensors, and so on). This implies that the user can engage in real-time with an always-present environment that he can access whenever he wishes.

Many proponents think that in the ideal future version of "The Metaverse," there would be a single platform where you could link your persona, identity, and platform services, and many worlds would be developed to which you could obtain access. Like a world with multiple sub-worlds which you can create, join, or leave. Important factors are a definition for digital identity, digital currencies, digital ownership, and the universal transferability of digital assets, thus enabling a fully functioning economy in a virtual world.

The Metaverse might thus replace various parts of tourism, such as what it means to attend a concert, locate art exhibitions, and, most importantly, how people learn, study, connect, and even meet up with friends.

Evolution from Web 1, Web 2, Web 3 to the Metaverse

There is a lot of debate over the definitions of Web3 and the distinction between it and the Metaverse, even if there is no clear agreement. Many crypto fans feel that crypto is the next stage of the internet, while others argue that after the social interaction-based Web2, the immersive Internet known as the "Metaverse" will emerge. It is unclear where the line should be drawn and where distinctions should be made, but the debate over whether Web3 is blockchain and crypto or immersive internet with virtual worlds will continue.

CHAPTER 1

WHAT DOES 'METAVERSE' REALLY MEAN?

T he Metaverse is a 3D, permanent, online ecosystem that connects a various virtual worlds. It may be compared to a future version of the internet. Thanks to the Metaverse, users will be able to collaborate, meet, play games, and interact in these 3D spaces.

While the Metaverse as a whole does not yet exist, metaverse-like components may be found on a number of platforms. Currently, video games provide the most realistic metaverse experience. Developers have stretched the bounds of what a game can be by staging in-game events and creating virtual economies.

Cryptocurrencies can be a great complement for a metaverse, even if they aren't required. They make it possible to build a digital economy based on a variety of utility tokens and virtual valuables (NFTs). Adopting crypto wallets like Trust Wallet and MetaMask would also assist the Metaverse. Furthermore, blockchain technology can create reliable and transparent governance systems.

Existing blockchain-based, metaverse-like apps offer people liveable earnings. Many people utilize Axie Infinity as a play-to-earn game to supplement their income. SecondLive and Decentraland are two other successful examples of merging the blockchain realm with virtual reality apps.

The world's biggest IT companies are attempting to lead the route for the future. However, the decentralized nature of the blockchain sector enables smaller players to participate in the development of Metaverse.

The virtual, physical, and financial worlds are all becoming increasingly intertwined. At the touch of a button, the devices we use to govern our lives provide us access to almost anything we want. This has had an impact on the crypto sector as well. Crypto aficionados are no longer the only ones that use NFTs, crypto payments, and blockchain games. As part of a growing metaverse, they are now all readily available.

The Metaverse is a concept for an online, 3D virtual world that brings people from all walks of life together. It would connect several platforms in the same way that the internet links multiple websites with a single browser.

Snow Crash, a science-fiction novel by Neal Stephenson, established the idea. While the notion of a metaverse was formerly thought to be science fiction, it now looks to be a possibility in the future.

AR will power the Metaverse, with each user controlling a character or avatar. For instance, you can take a mixed reality meeting with an Oculus VR headset in your virtual workplace, finish work, then relax in a blockchain-based game, and manage your crypto finances and portfolio all inside the Metaverse.

6

Some aspects of the Metaverse may already be seen in virtual video game environments. Games like Second Life and Fortnite and work socializing tools like Gather.town bring many aspects of our life together in virtual worlds. These apps aren't quite as sophisticated as the Metaverse; however, they are close. The Metaverse doesn't yet exist.

In addition to social media and gaming, the Metaverse will include economics, decentralized government, digital identities, and other applications. User-created valuable goods and currencies continue to contribute in the development of a single, united metaverse. Because of these characteristics, blockchain appears to be a suitable contender for powering this future technology.

What does the Metaverse have to do with video games?

Video games now deliver the closest metaverse experience because of 3D virtual reality.

This isn't solely because they're 3D. Video games now include services and features that apply to various areas of our lives. Roblox is a video game that offers virtual events such as concerts and meetups. Players no longer simply play the game; they also use it in "cyberspace" for other activities and aspects of their lives. In the online game Fortnite, for example, Travis Scott's virtual in-game music tour garnered 12.3 million players.

What role does cryptocurrency play in the Metaverse?

The 3D aspect of the Metaverse is provided by gaming, but it falls short of providing all of the requirements for a virtual environment that can cover all aspects of life. Other essential components, like digital proof of ownership, governance, accessibility, and value transfer, can be provided by crypto. But what do these mean exactly?

If we interact, work, or even purchase virtual items in the Metaverse in the future, we'll need a secure means to establish ownership. We must also feel safe when moving these objects and money across the Metaverse. Finally, if the Metaverse becomes so significant in our lives, we will want to be involved in decision-making.

Although several video games already have rudimentary solutions, many developers prefer to employ crypto and blockchain as a superior alternative. While the creation of video games is more regulated, blockchain allows for a transparent and decentralized approach to dealing with the issues.

Blockchain developers are influenced by the video game industry as well. Gamification is common in Gamefi and Decentralized Finance (DeFi). There appear to be enough commonalities between the two worlds in the future for them to become even more interwoven. The following are the key aspects of blockchain that make it suitable for the Metaverse:

1. Digital proof of ownership: If you have a wallet and access to your private keys, you can instantly verify ownership of a blockchain

activity or asset. For instance, you might display an exact transcript of your transactions on the blockchain while at work to demonstrate accountability. One of the most dependable methods to establish a digital identity and offer proof of ownership is to use a wallet.

2. Digital collectibility: Just as we can prove who owns an item, we can also prove that it is original and unique. For a metaverse that wishes to integrate more real-world action, this is crucial. Using NFTs, we can create products that are completely unique and cannot be replicated or produced. A blockchain can also be used to indicate the ownership of tangible assets.

3. Value transfer: A metaverse will need a safe transfer method that consumers can trust. In-game currency in multiplayer games is less secure than crypto on a blockchain. If users spend a lot of time in the Metaverse and even generate money there, they'll require a reliable currency.

4. Governance: Users should determine the rules that govern their interactions with the Metaverse. We can vote in corporations and elect presidents and governments in the real world. Fair governance will be essential in the Metaverse, and blockchain is already a proven approach.

5. Accessibility: Anyone in the world can create a wallet on public blockchains. Unlike a bank account, you do not need to pay any money or disclose any information. Therefore, it is one of the easiest methods to handle funds and a digital identity online.

6. Interoperability: Blockchain technology enhances the interoperability of diverse systems all the time. Avalanche (AVAX) and Polkadot (DOT) are two projects that allow you to create unique blockchains that can communicate with one another. Multiple projects will need to be linked in a single metaverse, and blockchain technology can help with that.

What is a metaverse job?

As previously stated, the Metaverse will bring all facets of life together in one place. While many people today work from home, you'll be able to visit a 3D office and interact with your coworkers' avatars in the Metaverse. Your employment might potentially be metaverse-related, allowing you to earn money that you can use in the Metaverse. In reality, jobs of this nature already exist in some manner.

GameFi and other play-to-earn models are now allowing people all around the world to earn a stable income. These online jobs are great candidates for future metaverse implementation because they prove that people are willing to spend time living and working in virtual worlds. Examples of Play-to-earn games that lack avatars or 3D worlds include Axie Infinity and Gods Unchained. It is the notion, though, that they could be a part of the Metaverse as a means to make money fully online.

Metaverse examples

While there isn't currently a single, linked metaverse, several platforms and initiatives are comparable to the Metaverse. These generally incorporate NFTs and other blockchain features. Consider the three examples below:

SecondLive

SecondLive is a 3D virtual world where users can socialize, learn, and do business by controlling avatars. A NFT marketplace for trading collectibles is also part of the idea.

Axie Infinity

Axie Infinity is a play-to-earn game that has allows players in developing countries to earn a steady income. A player can start farming the Smooth Love Potion (SLP) token by acquiring or receiving three creatures known as Axies. If someone sold their tickets on the open market, they might make anywhere from $200 to $1000 (USD), depending on how much they played and the market price.

While Axie Infinity doesn't include any 3D characters or avatars, it does enable users to operate in a metaverse-like setting. You may have heard the famous story of Filipinos utilizing it as a substitute for full-time work or welfare.

Decentraland

Decentraland is a virtual world that blends social components, cryptocurrencies, and non-fungible tokens with virtual real estate. Furthermore, players participate actively in the platform's governance. NFTs are utilized to represent cosmetic collectibles in NFTs, as they are in other blockchain games. They're also utilized for LAND, which are 16x16 meter land parcels that players can buy with MANA in the game. All of these work together to create a complex crypto-economy.

What does the Metaverse's future hold?

Facebook is one of the most vocal proponents of a unified metaverse. This is particularly intriguing for a crypto-powered metaverse due to Facebook's Diem stablecoin project. Mark Zuckerberg has declared unequivocally that he aims to launch a metaverse project to promote remote work and create financial opportunities for individuals in developing countries. Because Facebook owns social media, communication, and cryptocurrency platforms, it is in a great position to bring these worlds together. Other significant IT companies researching the creation of a metaverse include Microsoft, Apple, and Google.

The next step toward a crypto-powered metaverse looks to be deeper integration between NFT marketplaces and 3D virtual worlds. NFT holders may already sell their items on marketplaces like OpenSea and BakerySwap, but no widely utilized 3D platform exists yet. On a larger scale, blockchain developers could create successful metaverse-like products with a larger organic user base than a huge tech company.

While a unified metaverse is likely a long way off, we can already identify trends that might lead to its establishment. It seems like yet another sci-fi use case for cryptocurrencies and blockchain technology. It's unclear whether we'll ever truly arrive at a metaverse. However, in the meantime, we can already participate in metaverse-like initiatives and continue to integrate blockchain into our daily lives.

CHAPTER 2

METAVERSE POTENTIALS

F acebook just changed its name to Meta, and Meta has unveiled the Metaverse as a first step. However, it appears that many people have brushed the Metaverse under the rug (or haven't, which is why you got this book).

If Meta's claims regarding the Metaverse are true, it has the ability to influence our future in a variety of ways. That is why we have decided to write a whole post explaining its potential and its possible benefits and drawbacks.

In basic terms, Metaverse is a shared, perpetual virtual universe. This is an idea that enables you to achieve almost whatever you want. It's similar to immersing oneself in virtual reality and acting as if you're there.

You can design your reality and live in it in this new virtual universe. You can theoretically act as though you're in New York City while in Cape Town, South Africa. You can make your character a pilot and fly planes worldwide while working as a banker in the back of a counter in real life.

The point is that the Metaverse will allow you to create the world you want to live in and then live in it digitally. Within your newly made fantasy world, you can almost be anyone or whatever you choose.

And how will Meta go about accomplishing this? Through Augmented Reality (AR) and Virtual Reality (VR). And Meta will cover the expense, allowing many individuals on the earth to participate in the Metaverse.

Based on the preceding description, the Metaverse is a fairly fascinating technology. However, there are advantages and disadvantages like any other cutting-edge technology. Let's begin with the positives.

The Metaverse's Potential Benefits

The Metaverse has a lot of potential benefits, and we'll start with the first one that comes to mind: "Experience."

1. Experience

You can be anybody you want and go wherever you want in the Metaverse. You can live out your thoughts and dreams. In this environment, you receive a whole new level of experience.

For example, you could opt to play the part of the finest chef in the world in the morning and then go surfing in the tropics of the Bahamas in the afternoon. All of this is possible to do from the comfort of your own home, and it seems very real. This gets us to the second positive.

2. Expression

Metaverse Avatar

We have profile images, sometimes known as DPs, for our social media accounts. When someone visits our profile, this is the first thing they see. However, you will get an Avatar in the Metaverse instead of a DP.

An avatar is a 3D representation of oneself. You can, however, create and alter it to suit your needs. You have the ability to increase your height, add weight, and wear whatever style of clothing you like. You can be any gender, race, or even an animal you desire.

According to the report, the avatars would not appear like cartoons but rather like live pictures of oneself. And this will give it a more realistic feel. Simply said, you will not feel trapped in the body into which you were born. This is a whole new level of communicating with others.

People born with severe impairments, for example, can simply remove their disabilities. These folks can quickly construct the version of themselves that they have always imagined. This takes us to another intriguing Metaverse benefit: "Teleportation."

3. Teleportation

You can create your own house, design a workspace, and invite people over in the Metaverse. If you think video calls are amazing, you'll love the concept of Teleportation in the Metaverse.

Consider creating your own virtual home or office area and inviting people to join you. They'll be able to join with their near-live avatar, and you'll all be able to sit and talk in the virtual environment like actual people.

This means that teleportation in the Metaverse is as easy as clicking a link. You can simply establish the place and invite people to join by sending the URL. It's that easy and quick.

4. Knowledge and Study

Before Google, we gathered information and learned new things by reading books from the library. On the other hand, Google came along and delivered everything to you with a single click of a button via Google search. Google may well be replaced by the Metaverse.

You can learn about objects in the Metaverse by touching and gazing at them. And this data will be presented to you more visibly and engagingly. You can also choose to learn about things by traveling to any location and at any time.

Learning things faster also allows you to complete tasks more quickly. This leads us to another Metaverse benefit.

5. Fast and Improved Productivity

The Metaverse's productivity will not just be faster but also better. Thanks to technology, you'll be able to work from wherever you choose. You can choose to be in a quiet spot if you enjoy quietness. Or perhaps you enjoy listening to music while working? It is entirely up to you to create that atmosphere.

The point is that you get to choose the environment you want to work in. In addition, the Metaverse is said to have a speedier input system.

Instead of typing on a keyboard or writing with a pen, you can enter text using your voice, gestures, or simply your thoughts. On the other hand, the last one is still a work in progress, and we have a long way to go before we get there.

Meta is actively developing an electromyography (EMG) system for input devices. This technology can identify and intercept nerve impulses from what you're telling it. Using this technology, your fingertips can virtually write what your brain tells them to write (you might want to read this point again).

6. Safer Environment

Carbon dioxide emissions from businesses and cars are serious environmental issues. However, with the Metaverse, this will change for the better. For one thing, you won't be driving actual automobiles as often, which means less carbon dioxide will be emitted.

Furthermore, Metaverse's virtual teleportation capability eliminates the necessity for automobiles. So, will this imply fewer manufacturing enterprises and lower CO_2 emissions in our environment? Possibly.

The greater the number of people who join the Metaverse, the more likely they will buy digital items to improve their experience. As a result, there may be fewer automobiles, aircraft, trucks, and other vehicles.

7. New Economy

The Horizon market place is a new metaverse market place that Meta is building. This is a marketplace where anyone with coding abilities may sell their products. You can charge people to test virtual clothing or even new virtual experiences that you design.

Material limitations will not be an issue. All you'll need are some coding abilities and some creativity. As a result, a whole new set of people will profit from the Metaverse. You can virtually take your company to the Metaverse and meet many clients.

To be honest, the entire Metaverse concept is very interesting. It allows you to be with anybody, create and experience anything, and even make money by selling digital products. You're in the middle of a vast universe. However, it has its own set of potential drawbacks, the most prominent being "addiction."

Potential Negatives of the Metaverse

1. Addiction

You know how we complain about people spending too much time on the internet watching movies, playing games, making TikTok videos, and even streaming videos? The concept of the Metaverse, on the other hand, will greatly intensify this.

Consider this: who wants to rush out of a setting he or she created that appears to be perfect? I mean, the person is living his or her fantasies, has the ideal figure, travels to the most prestigious locations, and does whatever he or she wants.

It's all too simple to lose touch with reality and start preferring to stay in the virtual world, even over your personal life. Adults may be victims of this as well, and in the end, we might need some a slew of restrictions to keep things in check.

When we talk about addiction as an issue, we get to the Metaverse's second possible negative.

2. Inferiority Complex and Depression

We've already seen how images on social media make individuals detest certain parts of their bodies. Plastic surgery to fix portions of the body has become more popular among teenagers throughout the world in recent years. But what if you live in a dream world where you create the perfect physique and then return to reality to discover that you're still the same person?

It's simple: when you exit the Metaverse and find you're not who you imagined yourself to be in the virtual world, you get a reality check. You're still not as tall or as chubby as you desire in real life. Depression will gradually set in, causing you to spend more time in the Metaverse than in reality.

I'm not saying it has to happen, but the potential remains. Consider a real-life person with a serious health problem. He has eradicated such a situation in the Metaverse, and everything appears to be great, but what happens when he exits the virtual universe? Reality check.

3. Data and Security

Access to and exchange of data is another possible drawback of this world. Joining the Metaverse, after all, will need sharing a massive quantity of data with Meta. On a far wider scale, this includes, but is not limited to, your behaviors, interests, patterns, and so on.

And, based on the past, Meta isn't particularly effective at data management. And disclosing all of this information is not a smart idea. What if there's a data breach and someone else gets their hands on your data? It's rather frightening.

4. Denying Reality

You can build your reality in the Metaverse, but who decides what is genuine and what isn't? I mean, a user can choose to remove genuine things from their Metaverse simply because they don't like them, not because they aren't real.

If you don't like people from a given tribe, you might elect to remove them from your Metaverse. You can decide to remove homeless people or hospitals if you don't like them. The point is that people might simply deny reality and create a parallel universe in the Metaverse, which is a concern.

What exactly is the issue here? They'll have to cope with these issues after they emerge from the virtual world. They can't stay in the virtual world indefinitely (or can they?).

5. Moderation

Who is going to regulate this virtual reality for racism or hate speech? What method will be used to carry out the moderation? I mean, monitoring social media sites is hard enough, but regulating an entire world made by various individuals takes it to a whole new level.

Will Meta monitor each user, catching every single motion, character, word, and text that promotes hatred, racism, fake news, and online bullying? Meta will require a massive workforce to do this, and even then, it will be extremely tough.

And if moderation isn't done correctly, the entire virtual world may quickly devolve into pandemonium. I mean, not everyone will be there only to spread good feelings.

After all, we're still people, and we'll have to eat, drink, and sleep in the real world. So, even if we construct a beautiful world in the Metaverse, we'll have to return to reality and live our lives.

Meta's proposal is intriguing, and it appears to be the way social media will evolve in the future, allowing users to engage more authentically. You have complete freedom to be whatever you want, do anything you want, and go wherever you choose.

However, it also magnifies the drawbacks of social media use, such as harassment, depression, addiction, and even security concerns. And 5G connectivity's speed is the primary reason why this entire virtual world appears to be viable.

Can you image trying to access such a universe via 2G or 3G? It would be extremely difficult to use only because of the buffering. Development in one field of technology inevitably leads to advancement in others.

So, while we're all ecstatic with the new Metaverse concept, it's equally fine to consider the drawbacks. We'll be able to better prepare ourselves for "The Future of Social Media" in this way.

CHAPTER 3

FUTURE OF THE METAVERSE ECONOMY

The Metaverse has gone from literary text rumination to boundless digital actuality in the previous year. The Metaverse is an interactive, digital alternative to the real world, where virtual avatars come together to shop, play, work, pursue hobbies, or otherwise assemble to engage in online communities and explore the digital space. The term fully entered the mainstream when Facebook changed itself to Meta Platforms Inc. (now popularly referred to as Meta) in October 2021 in a bid to go beyond its social media beginnings and announce a larger plan around "the next chapter of the Internet."

Both outsiders and industry insiders are baffled by the notion, not least because the corporations constructing the metaverse claim it will take years and billions of dollars to actualize. On the other hand, the Metaverse will already be becoming more solid in the new year, as it strives to prove its promised potential. Players in the Metaverse will need to address three frontiers to advance to the next stage of development: obtaining skilled talent, making significant investment moves, and pushing the bounds on creative experiences.

Securing skilled talent

Meta is actively recruiting from various places, including Apple's Silicon Valley neighbor and other West Coast tech titan Microsoft. It has poached most of the 100 workers who left the HoloLens augmented reality headset team last year. Though sales were slow to take off, Microsoft's HoloLens was one of the first AR devices on the market, making its employees highly sought-after metaverse talent. Meta has also stated that it would recruit 10,000 engineers in Europe to help construct the next Internet frontier. It will be tough for them to follow through on their promise to hire AR/VR experts in an already short on IT expertise.

Meta is far not the only proponent of the Metaverse, despite being one of the most visible and opinionated. Nvidia, a chipmaker, has also focused on the Metaverse, although they've dubbed it "omniverse." Nvidia has created a subscription service called Omniverse Enterprise that allows producers, designers, and others to interact in a shared online simulation environment. BMW, for example, uses Omniverse Enterprise to replicate its manufacturing operations as part of its smart manufacturing initiatives. Meanwhile, Nvidia's demand for competent omniverse engineers increases because processors are the Metaverse's images and animation lifeblood.

Gaming businesses, which have long been pioneering immersive online experiences, are contenders for a front-row seat in the Metaverse. Roblox and Epic Games' smash Fortnite have already built large followings and in-game online economies, putting them in a good position to profit today. The issue isn't that gaming firms can't get people to play their games; they can't find qualified people to hire, which makes the hiring process even more difficult.

Making decisive investment moves

Another metaverse-induced trend that has lately made the news is gaming company mergers. Microsoft recently revealed intentions to buy Activision Blizzard, the creator of World of Warcraft and Candy Crash, for $69 billion in cash, hoping that best-selling games can entice skeptics to the Metaverse. These developments come after Take-Two revealed that it would purchase Farmville creator Zynga for $13 billion and, after 2021, witnessed a record $117 billion in-game acquisitions.

If chipmakers achieve their potential as metaverse powerhouses, they must also make the necessary investments. Intel stated that it would spend $20 billion on two manufacturing units in Ohio, with the potential for this investment to grow to $100 billion for eight manufacturing plants if things go well.

Walmart's New Store Design Is Another 'Wake-Up' Call for Department Stores

Investors, both institutional and retail, are preparing for the Metaverse. SoftBank made a $150 million investment in a South Korean metaverse platform in late November 2021. The stock prices of firms at the forefront of the industry have risen dramatically. Several metaverse-focused exchange-traded funds have emerged, with some displaying promise. Investors' desire for the Metaverse will grow as its vision develops.

The metaverse real estate market is on the more imaginative end of the investing spectrum. The cofounder of digital real estate business Metaverse Group, Michael Gord, told the New York Times, "Imagine if you arrived in New York when it was farmland and had the chance to acquire a block of SoHo." In the immersive online environment, Gord and other investors are speculating on property parcels. Virtual developers can create and rent out digital malls in virtual environments like Decentraland and Sandbox. One such developer paid $4.3 million for a home they bought from Atari, a video game business. Property transactions in the other world have soared, and the competition for valuable real estate will heat up even more in the next year, although many are wary of the volatile nature of digital real estate.

Taking innovative experiences to new heights

When organizations have the expertise and resources to establish and develop a world without boundaries, their imaginations can run wild as pioneers create the Metaverse's revolutionary experiences that will make up the Metaverse.

New metaverse experiences will reshape the future of employment. Aside from Nvidia's Omniverse Enterprise, Microsoft's Mesh and Meta's Horizon Workrooms are also designed to empower virtual work, with both allowing remote collaboration across devices via mixed reality apps. Bill Gates thinks that virtual meetings will migrate to the Metaverse within three years and that people would increasingly rely on VR gear and avatars at work. As a result, the role of corporate real estate could take another hit, empowering multiple generations of people who are already accustomed to working from home thanks to Covid to demand even more spatial flexibility in their work lives, with the Metaverse further reducing the need for a formal workplace.

School and social life will change as well. For example, Roblox intends to introduce instructional videogames to classrooms. Community-based metaverse experiences are enabled via platforms like AltspaceVR, which allow people to gather for live virtual events like comedy clubs or bar nights. Roblox envisions itself as a future center for metaverse events such as concerts, in addition to games. (For reference, recent Marshmello performance in Fortnite drew ten million people.)

Stores selling anything from fantasy digital critters to e-pparel might usher in a new age of business. Digital skins have long been popular in Fortnite, and more traditional stores follow suit. Balenciaga, Luis Vuitton, and Luxury labels Gucci are starting to sell e-clothing and e-bags, while Nike has filed trademarks for virtual gear, shoes, and accessories. For your virtual estate, you could even purchase a $650,000 digital yacht or NFT paintings. Meta-malls are starting to show up, allowing you to shop in virtual reality stores and stock up on avatar clothing.

While believers can't get enough of the Metaverse, skeptics may find that it's going too quickly. The FTC, for example, is throwing roadblocks in Meta's path by prolonging its antitrust investigation into previous VR transactions. The Metaverse, according to Chinese officials, has to be properly watched. Expensive headsets, as well as the unknown mental and physical health consequences of spending huge amounts of time wearing a headset and moving around in a parallel reality, might be a hurdle to popular adoption. Despite this, the tech sector remains firm in its trust in the Metaverse, estimating that it will be worth $800 billion by 2024 and have a population of one billion by 2030.

CHAPTER 4

HOW TO INVEST IN METAVERSE

S now Crash, Neal Stephenson's third novel, was published in 1992. In it, Stephenson's characters interact in a wholly digital world where looks may be modified on a whip, and digital real estate is just as valuable as actual land. Stephenson dubbed his virtual world "the Metaverse."

Public enterprises such as Meta (previously Facebook) and decentralized autonomous organizations (DAOs) such as the Decentraland Foundation have been working to make the Metaverse a financial reality for the past twenty-eight years. As a result, r gamers, digital collectors, retail investors, and developers all have access to whole new revenue streams.

It's worth noting, though, that the Metaverse is still in its early stages, and its value proposition has yet to be validated. Any metaverse investment should be viewed as speculative and high-risk.

Metaverse stocks

Investing in publicly listed firms whose business strategies or profitability are related to the Metaverse is the least volatile option for ordinary investors looking to purchase into the Metaverse. The list includes:

Meta Platforms Inc (NASDAQ: FB) - Mark Zuckerberg stated in October that the firm formerly known as Facebook Inc. would be rebranded as Meta Platforms Inc. Since the announcement, Meta has created Horizon Worlds, a virtual reality metaverse platform. The Oculus Quest 2 VR headset from Meta was also one of the most popular holiday presents. However, it remains to be seen whether higher headset purchases will increase Horizon Worlds users.

Roblox (NYSE: RBLX) - This is an online metaverse platform that enables users to build and share virtual environments. Since its debut in 2006, Roblox has developed significantly, with 24 million unique digital experiences, 9.5 million independent creators, 49.4 million daily active users - an increase of 35% year over year. Despite these figures, the business has yet to make a profit.

Boeing (NYSE: BA) utilizes the Metaverse to enhance and expand its manufacturing capabilities. In an interview with Reuters, Greg Hyslop, Boeing's top engineer, said that the jet maker intends to develop a proprietary digital environment where its human, computer, and robot employees can interact and collaborate seamlessly across the globe.

Microsoft (NASDAQ: MSFT) is attempting to carve out a metaverse niche in the business sector. According to the business, mesh for Microsoft Teams will be available in 2022. Individuals will create individualized avatars and work in a holographic 3D world that crosses geographic boundaries using the add-on to the popular video conferencing platform. Holoportation, a mechanism that enables users to access the previously described digital environment with a VR headset, will be a fundamental element of Microsoft Mesh. The user is represented as a realistic digital version of themselves, with the ability to communicate with team members as if they were in person.

Metaverse Land

Although the Metaverse is still in its early stages, platforms such as The Decentraland and Sandbox have already begun selling digital real estate in the form of NFTs, which are digital tokens on blockchain networks that may represent a broad range of unique items. When someone buys a piece of metaverse land, the metaverse platform's blockchain network validates the transaction and transfer of ownership.

The owner of the metaverse land NFT can rent, sell, or develop on his digital property once it has been acquired. Atari, a Japanese video game company, has bought 20 digital land plots in Decentraland and launched its crypto casino. Gamblers can place bets and get wins in crypto tax-free using the Atari token, which is based on the ERC20 standard. Atari has also revealed that in 2022, it will open its virtual hotel complex.

How to purchase metaverse land and other digital stuff

Several metaverse systems have built marketplaces where users can purchase and trade NFTs representing digital land and other items. Here's how to go about it.

A user who wants to buy metaverse real estate must first decide on which platform he wants to buy digital land. The Sandbox and Decentraland are two popular options, but there are more. Do your homework before purchasing any metaverse land.

The user must first establish a digital cryptocurrency wallet, a sort of computer program that connects to a blockchain network and saves cryptocurrency, while being compatible with the metaverse platform's blockchain.

After that, the buyer must go to his selected metaverse platform's marketplace and link his digital wallet to it.

At this point, acquiring digital land appears to be quite similar to owning land in the actual world. A buyer should consider the price, location, and future worth of the digital land he wants to acquire.

Once a buyer has found a plot of land, he must obtain the tokens or coins necessary to purchase it and put them in his digital wallet. The type of token or currency required to complete the transaction differs depending on the metaverse platform. For example, to buy digital land in Decentraland, a user would need to buy MANA tokens. SAND tokens would be required to purchase land in The Sandbox.

If the buyer has already linked and financed his digital wallet with the metaverse marketplace, all he has to do now is put a bid on the land or purchase it outright. The land's cost will be deducted from the digital wallet, and the NFT representing the land will be transferred to the user's wallet.

Buying additional metaverse NFT items, such as clothes and accessories for avatars, follows the same procedure.

Metaverse cryptocurrency

Metaverse initiatives on blockchain networks are powered by fungible tokens – divisible tokens that can be mutually exchanged. These tokens are used to buy digital assets such as virtual land and avatar outfit. They can also be exchanged for other cryptocurrencies or fiat currencies. Certain metaverse cryptocurrencies also allow its owners to vote on metaverse platform choices such as where money should be invested or which new features should be released first.

In theory, if the value of digital assets rises, so would the value of their associated tokens. Furthermore, certain metaverse platforms, such as Decentraland, burn all MANA tokens used to buy digital assets, thus removing them from circulation and raising the value of the remaining tokens.

The tokens in the Metaverse are listed below in descending order by market capitalization (market cap). These investments are inherently risky and should be seen as speculative. As a general guideline, you should never invest more money than you can afford to lose.

Decentraland (MANA) - Decentraland's MANA token drives the Decentraland metaverse and is used as a means of exchange on the platform's marketplace, with a market valuation of roughly $6 billion at the time of writing.

Axie Infinity (AXS) - Axie Infinity is a governance token, unlike Decentraland's MANA, which is used to buy digital products and services. Axie Infinity owners will vote on proposed choices that would affect the ecosystem, such as how funds in the community treasury are used. The AXS token will be modified in the future to allow it to be used to buy digital products and services on Axie Infinity.

The Sandbox (SAND) - Like Roblox, The Sandbox is centered on a metaverse of user-generated content. People who participate in The Sandbox's alpha user testing receive the SAND token. SAND tokens can also be bought on digital exchanges. SAND is a token that may be used for utility, governance, and staking. SAND holders can use it to purchase digital goods and services, vote on proposed projects inside The Sandbox, and stake their SAND for further benefits.

Enjin Coin (ENJ) - This is a blockchain-based gaming platform. Unlike The Sandbox and Axie Infinity, which only offer a single metaverse product, Enjin provides a variety of interconnected play-to-earn gaming experiences to its consumers. Enjin is unusual because its native token, ENJ, is "injected" into every NFT created within its ecosystem, arguably giving digital assets real-world value.

Companies with a lot of money invested in the Metaverse are spending millions of dollars to persuade customers that the Metaverse is upon us. Will it, however, bring in a new age of broad acceptance and barrier-free digital contact, or will it remain a niche product for gamers and future tech enthusiasts? Only time will tell if this is true. For the time being, retail investors interested in Metaverse should look into these platforms and assess Metaverse's future value.

CHAPTER 5

UNDERSTANDING THE METAVERSE THROUGH REAL-WORLD EXAMPLES

The phrase "metaverse" has been tossed about in recent months, particularly when Facebook announced its rebranding as Meta. Meta is a social technology startup with the mission of "bringing the metaverse to life." Many people in the Metaverse were intrigued by this.

The name and concept aren't new in and of itself. Ideas and examples of the Metaverse have been around for several decades. The term "metaverse" was coined in Neal Stephenson's 1992 novel Snow Crash; the characters utilize computer avatars to explore a digital world or engage with one another to escape their dystopian reality.

David Gelernter initially proposed the concept of a digital twin, or a virtual duplicate of something that exists in real life, in his book Mirror Worlds in 1991. Dr. Michael Grieves, credited as the inventor of the digital twin software idea, first applied the digital twin concept to manufacturing in 2002. In 2010, NASA employed digital twin technology to simulate space capsules.

The Metaverse appears to be upon us, but what is it, and what influence may it have on our daily lives?

Here are some examples that help you understand the Metaverse, how it works, and where it could be heading in the future.

It's difficult to narrow down a precise definition of the Metaverse.

The Metaverse is a loosely defined virtual universe where users have access to digital avatars that allow them to "live" in this virtual reality. People can communicate with friends, acquire and sell digital assets, go to virtual places (which may be entirely imagined or have real-life counterparts), and more in the Metaverse.

The Metaverse offers a world of limitless possibilities, similar to the OASIS in Ready Player One, where the user's imagination is the only restriction.

To put it another way, the Metaverse is a virtual universe that exists in addition to or as an extension of our physical reality. It's made up of interoperable technologies like augmented reality and virtual reality, and it works on a functional digital economy fueled by digital currencies or cryptocurrencies—and no, cryptocurrencies and digital currencies are not the same things.

Furthermore, there is no single, distinct metaverse. There are a lot of iterations in the Metaverse. For example, if you're playing Fortnite, you can enter a metaverse. If you use Facebook Horizon, you can also access a distinct metaverse. The Metaverse, on the other hand, is designed to be interoperable, which means you'll ultimately be able to access assets acquired on one platform and utilize them on another.

Examples of the Metaverse to Help Explain It

The Metaverse's premise and the possibilities it opens up are just incredible. Here are some real-world instances of the Metaverse and where it will help better describe this alternate reality.

The Metaverse in Pop Culture

• Ready Player One

Ready Player One is almost always used as an example when discussing the Metaverse. There is, however, a valid explanation for this. Ernest Cline's science fiction novel from 2011 presents a vivid image of what the Metaverse may look like and how it might function.

In the novel, set in 2045, people turn to the OASIS, a massively multiplayer online simulation game (MMOSG) with its virtual world (and currency) where they can interact with other players, visit different places, play games, and even shop, to escape a world ravaged by war, poverty, and climate change. The OASIS is a world where anything can happen—people's imaginations only constrain "reality," and anybody maybe whatever they wish.

If all of that is too much for you, watch the 2018 Steven Spielberg film adaptation, which provides a decent look at the book's Metaverse.

Facebook is well on its way to launching Facebook Horizon, its own version of the OASIS in the real world. The Oculus Rift or the Oculus Quest 2 headgear must enter this virtual world. Users can explore, create, play, and engage with other players in this vast digital environment.

• Fortnite Concerts

What began as a game has swiftly evolved into something more complex and capable of providing a wider range of experiences.

Players in Fortnite can construct their worlds and embark on adventures. They can play with other Fortnite gamers in the community. The game's crossplay feature allows users to play it on various platforms, including Xbox, Playstation, PC, and mobile phones.

Fortnite has evolved into more than just a game, with players able to hang out and attend in-game concerts. Ariana Grande, Marshmello, and Travis Scott were among the artists who performed. Fortnite's developer, Epic Games, raises the stakes by launching the Soundwave Series, which includes music from musicians all around the world. The Series gives gamers access to in-game interactive activities.

Games and Social Networks in the Metaverse

• Second Life

Second Life is an online environment where users can create digital avatars, explore the world, connect with other users, and sell products and services using the Linden Dollar, the in-world currency.

Second Life is a forerunner of the Metaverse, in which users can interact with one another and the digital world in a shared virtual realm. It has been around since the late 2000s and allows users to explore the Metaverse's potential.

• The Sandbox

The Sandbox is a virtual metaverse where people can create and play in virtual worlds. It also allows individuals to control and profit from their in-game experiences. NFTs can be used to buy and trade lands and assets in The Sandbox metaverse.

NFTs are virtual tokens that are generated on the blockchain. This makes them unique, indivisible, and non-transferable, allowing you to own your in-game assets digitally.

This shows the Metaverse's rising acceptance of digital currencies. In a digital future, we will be able to view, utilize, and define money in ways that are currently unimaginable.

• Illuvium

Illuvium is a 2022 release described as an open-world roleplaying game based on the Ethereum Blockchain. Illuvials are deity-like creatures housed on Shards, and players seek and catch them here. Players in Illuvium essentially gather NFTs, which symbolize each Illuvial. You'll also be able to accumulate in-game products that you may sell on third-party NFT marketplaces.

Augmented Reality (AR)

AR is a technology that mixes real-world aspects with digital augmentation. For instance, you could be in the actual world yet see a dragon perched on your neighbor's car when using augmented reality.

It's already utilized in a lot of games and navigation systems. Pokémon Go is one of the most popular AR applications, allowing users to search for, fight against, and capture Pokémon that "appear" in the real world via their phone's camera.

In addition to gaming applications, AR is also employed in navigation systems. Google's AR and VR technologies allow users to explore the actual world more.

This real-world app aims to provide users with a more immersive experience, allowing them to get the most out of their smart devices. For instance, when you use Google Maps' Live View, you can traverse an area more easily because directions are overlaid on your Google Street View images.

Another use is the ability to employ augmented reality in Google Search. This allows you to set 3D objects in your area and better understand their scale.

Other real-world applications of augmented reality include:

Giving you a sense of what a piece of furniture may look like in your home

Being used in football games to illustrate plays

Bringing historical locations to life by overlaying ancient civilizations over ruins

AR technology is also finding its way into the classroom. The Metaverse Studio is an augmented reality platform that allows teachers and students to develop augmented reality in their classrooms. It can build applications, games, and activities to supplement project-based learning.

Metaverse Real Estate

We can't talk about the Metaverse without including real estate applications. People purchase and sell homes on digital marketplaces just like they do in the real world. They are, however, trading with cryptocurrencies.

While metaverse real estate is still regarded as "extremely speculative," technologists predict the Metaverse will eventually have its own fully functioning economy. The popularity of virtual real estate has led to the sale of digital assets for millions of dollars. A plot of virtual property in Decentraland was sold for 618,000 mana ($2.4 million in crypto), while a parcel of virtual land in The Sandbox was sold for $4.3 million.

Because of the Metaverse's growing popularity, many businesses have decided to create their digital worlds and, with them, digital assets. The Metaverse Group, for example, operates Decentraland, a virtual environment that its users entirely control. Much like in other virtual worlds, users can explore lands owned by other users, create challenges and artwork, engage in events to earn rewards, and exchange digital goods using mana, Decentraland's sort of cryptocurrency.

SuperWorld, a virtual environment where you can buy, sell, and accumulate pieces of virtual land, is another outstanding example of real estate in the Metaverse. The Taj Mahal (50 EHT), the Eiffel Tower, and Mount Rushmore (0.1 ETH) are among the 64.8 billion distinct parcels of virtual property it has to date (selling for 100 ETH).

Users who buy a piece of virtual real estate become owners of unique digital assets and platform stakeholders who can share revenue generated by user activities on the property.

The Metaverse is gradually taking shape. It has found its way into various areas of our life, from games and movies to real-world navigation systems. While the Metaverse is difficult to describe and is still in its early phases of development, we can say for now that it is brimming with potential. What remains to be seen is what else the Metaverse has in store for us in the future.

CHAPTER 6

WEB 3.0

Web 3.0 is a hypothetical future version of the internet that is built on public blockchains, which are used to keep track of things like cryptocurrency transactions. Web 3.0 is good because it doesn't have to be run by anyone. Instead of people using services like Google, Facebook, and Apple to get on the internet, people control and regulate parts of the internet themselves.

Web 3.0 doesn't need "permission," which means that central authorities don't have the power to decide who can use what services. It also doesn't require "trust," which implies that virtual transactions between two or more parties don't need the use of an intermediary. Web 3.0 theoretically preserves user privacy better because these organizations and intermediaries conduct most of the data collecting.

Decentralized finance, or DeFi, is a Web 3.0 component that's gaining traction. It comprises using the blockchain to conduct real-world financial transactions without the involvement of banks or the government. Meanwhile, many significant businesses and venture capital firms are pouring money into Web 3.0, and it's difficult to imagine that their involvement won't lead to centralized power.

The evolution of the web

The World Wide Web is the primary instrument used by billions of people to trade, read, and write information and connect through the internet. People use the internet in very different ways now than they did in the early days, and the internet has changed a lot over the years. Web 1.0, Web 2.0, and Web 3.0 are 3 stages in the growth of the internet.

What is Web 1.0?

In the early days of the internet, Web 1.0 was the first version of the internet. So think of it as the read-only or syntactic web. Most of the participants were content consumers, whereas the creators were mostly web developers who built websites with mostly text or graphics-based content. Web 1.0 existed from 1991 to 2004.

In Web 1.0, sites delivered static content rather than dynamic hypertext markup language (HTML). There was limited interactivity on the web pages, and data and content came from a static file system rather than a database.

What is Web 2.0?

Most of us have only seen the web in its present form, often known as Web 2.0, or the interactive read-write and social web. In the Web 2.0 ecosystem, you do not have to be a developer to participate in the development process. Many apps are built so that anybody may become a creator.

You can think and share your ideas with the rest of the world. In Web 2.0, you can also share a video for millions of other people to view, interact with, and comment on. Web 2.0 apps include Youtube, Facebook, Flickr, Instagram, Twitter, and other social media platforms.

Companies can employ web technologies like HTML5, CSS3, and Javascript frameworks like AngularJs, ReactJs, VueJs, and others to build new ideas that enable users to contribute more to the Social Web. Because Web 2.0 is built around people, developers need to provide a method to empower and engage them.

Twitter, Instagram, YouTube, and LinkedIn were very different when they first came out. Now, they are very similar. The following is a typical procedure followed by all of these companies:

The company releases an app.

It enlists as many people as feasible.

The company then generates money from its user base.

The user experience is typically exceedingly sleek when a developer or organization develops a popular app, especially as the app's popularity rises. This is why they were able to get momentum so quickly in the first place. Many software companies are indifferent to monetization at first. Instead, they're completely focused on attracting and maintaining new customers, but they'll have to start making money someday.

However, the constraints of raising venture capital frequently affect the life cycle and, as a result, the user experience of many of the applications we use today. When a company gets venture capital to develop an app, investors often expect a return on investment in tens or hundreds of times their investment. This implies that the organization is typically driven into one of two paths: marketing or data sales, rather than adopting a long-term growth plan that can be supported organically.

More data equals better-targeted marketing for many Web 2.0 companies, such as Google, Facebook, Twitter, etc. This results to more clicks and, ultimately, more ad revenue. The centralization and exploitation of user data are necessary for the web to function as we know and use it today. As a result, data breaches in Web 2.0 apps are rather prevalent. There are even websites dedicated to tracking data breaches and telling you when your data has been compromised.

You have no control over your data or its storage in Web 2.0. Companies regularly track and keep user data without their knowledge or consent. This data is then owned and managed by the companies in charge of these platforms. Furthermore, governments often shut down servers or seize bank accounts when they suspect someone is expressing an opinion that opposes their propaganda. Governments can easily intervene, control, or shut down apps using centralized servers.

Governments regularly intervene in banks because banks are also computerized and centralized. They can, however, suspend bank accounts or restrict access to funds during periods of extreme volatility, excessive inflation, or other political upheaval. Web 3.0, which seeks to drastically rethink how we develop and interact with apps from the bottom up, will fix many of these issues.

What is Web 3.0?

Web 3.0, also known as read-write-execute or Semantic Web, is the age that refers to the web's future (starting in 2010). Machine Learning (ML) and Artificial Intelligence (AI) allow computers to evaluate data in the same manner that people do, allowing for the intelligent development and dissemination of valuable content tailored to the requirements of individual users.

Although both emphasise decentralisation, there are a few fundamental differences between Web 2.0 and Web 3.0. Applications that run on a single server or store data in a single database are rarely created and deployed by Web 3.0 developers (usually hosted on and managed by a single cloud provider).

Web 3.0 apps, on the other hand, are based on decentralized networks of many peer-to-peer nodes (servers), blockchains, or a combination of the two. Decentralized apps (DApps) are the word for these programs, and you'll hear it a lot in the Web 3.0 community. Participants in the network (developers) are rewarded for providing high-quality services to create a robust and secure decentralized network.

What is Web 3.0 in crypto?

When it comes to Web 3.0, you will often hear the term "cryptocurrency" mentioned. This is because many Web 3.0 protocols rely significantly on cryptocurrency. Instead, it provides monetary incentive (tokens) to everyone who wants to help establish, control, contribute to, or enhance. Web 3.0 tokens are digital assets linked to establishing a decentralized Internet. These protocols might provide services like compute, bandwidth, storage, identity, hosting, and other internet services that cloud companies provide.

For instance, the Ethereum-based Livepeer protocol serves as a marketplace for streaming applications and video infrastructure providers. Helium uses blockchains and tokens to reward consumers and small businesses for providing and confirming wireless coverage and transferring device data across the network.

People can earn money by participating in the protocol in various technical and non-technical ways. Consumers of the service often pay to utilize the protocol, similar to how they would pay an Amazon Web Services cloud provider. Unnecessary and usually wasteful intermediates are eliminated, as with many kinds of decentralization.

Furthermore, digital currencies, nonfungible tokens (NFTs), and other blockchain entities will be actively used in Web 3.0. For example, Reddit aims to break into Web 3.0 by creating a method that uses cryptocurrency tokens to allow users to effectively manage portions of the on-site communities in which they engage. According to the concept, users would earn "community points" by posting on a certain subreddit. Then, the user is awarded points based on the number of people who upvote or downvote a certain post. (It's essentially a blockchain-based Reddit Karma.)

Those points can be utilized as voting shares, giving users who have made large contributions a bigger say in the community's decisions. Because those points are stored on the blockchain, their owners have more control over them; they can't be simply taken away, and you can be tracked. This is only one application, a corporate version of the Web 3.0 idea of Decentralized Autonomous Organizations, which use tokens to distribute ownership and decision-making power more equally.

Web 2.0 vs Web 3.0

The transition from Web 2.0 to 3.0 is gradually and mostly unnoticed by the public. Web 3.0 apps appear and feel the same as 2.0 applications, but the backend is quite different.

The future of Web 3.0 is universal apps that can be read and used by various devices and software types, making our business and recreational activities easier.

Data decentralization and the creation of a transparent and secure environment will be enabled by the emergence of technologies such as distributed ledgers and blockchain storage, which will challenge Web 2.0's centralization, surveillance, and exploitative advertising.

People will completely control their data in a decentralized web when decentralized infrastructure and application platforms replace centralized tech enterprises.

Let's look at the 4 properties of Web 3.0 to better appreciate its complexity and intricacies.

Semantic web

The "semantic web" is an essential component of Web 3.0. The term was coined by Tim Berners-Lee to describe a data network that can be parsed by robots. So, what does that imply in simple English? What does the term "semantics" mean exactly? What's the difference between "I adore Bitcoin" and "I <3 Bitcoin"?

The meanings of the two phrases are comparable, despite the differences in syntax. In the above example, semantics is concerned with the meaning or emotion represented by facts, and both of those statements indicate the same emotions. Artificial intelligence and the semantic web are the two foundations of Web 3.0. The semantic web will assist in teaching the computer what the data means, enabling AI to generate real-world use cases for the data.

The fundamental idea is to create a knowledge spiderweb over the internet to assist people in understanding what words mean and in creating, sharing, and connecting content via search and analysis. Due to semantic information, Web 3.0 will allow for more data interchange.

As a result, the user experience progresses to a new level of connectivity that takes use of all accessible data.

3D graphics

As the internet evolves from a simple two-dimensional web to a more realistic three-dimensional cyberworld, Web 3.0 will significantly impact its future. 3D design is used extensively on Web 3.0 websites and services, such as online gaming, real estate, and e-commerce.

As strange as it may appear, thousands of individuals from all over the world are presently engaging in this area. Think of online games like World of Warcraft or Players in Second Life are significantly more concerned about the safety of their virtual avatars than their real-life counterparts.

Artificial Intelligence

Websites will be able to select and provide the most relevant content thanks to artificial intelligence. Organizations have begun to solicit client feedback in the present Web 2.0 age better to determine the quality of an asset or a product. Consider a site like Rotten Tomatoes, which allows people to score and review movies. Films having a better rating are commonly referred to as "good films." These kinds of lists enable us to skip the "poor data" and get right to the "good data."

As we've already said, peer reviews are one of Web 2.0's most important contributions. On the other hand, human suggestions are not incorruptible, as we all know. A group of people may band together to offer a film undeservedly positive reviews to boost their ratings. Artificial intelligence can learn to differentiate between good and poor data and provide us with reliable data.

Ubiquitous

The term "ubiquitous" relates to the notion of being or being present in several locations simultaneously, also known as "omnipresence." This feature is already available in Web 2.0. Consider Instagram, a social media platform where users may take photos with their phones and then publish and distribute them online, where they become their intellectual property. When a picture is shared, it becomes widely known and available.

The Web 3.0 experience will be accessible everywhere, at any time, thanks to the expansion of mobile devices and internet connections. As with Web 1.0 and Web 2.0, the internet will no longer be limited to your desktop computer or smartphone. It will be all-powerful and all-knowing. Because most items around you are linked online, Web 3.0 could be called the web of everything and everywhere (Internet of Things).

How can you prepare your brand for the Web 3.0 revolution?

Early-stage applications of the Spatial Web, also known as Web 3.0, are already available, as future as that seems. Now is the moment for CEOs to grasp what the next computer era entails, how it will affect businesses, and how it will generate new value as it evolves.

Furthermore, by evaluating existing and practical Web 3.0 business models, users must be prepared to understand how some of the more established and experimental Web 3.0 business models may accumulate value in the coming years. Below are some of the approaches.

Issuing a native asset

The value of these native assets comes from the security they provide, and they are necessary for the network's operation. By providing hashing power, to providing a high enough incentive for honest miners, the cost for malicious actors to carry out an attack rises in lockstep with the price of the native asset, and the added security drives further demand for the currency driving up its price and value. The value of these native assets has been carefully assessed and quantified.

Building a network by holding the native asset

Some of the earliest crypto network organizations had a single goal: to increase the profitability and value of their networks. "Grow their local asset treasury; construct the ecosystem" was the emerging economic plan. Blockstream depends on its BTC balance sheet to produce wealth as one of the major Bitcoin Core maintainers. Meanwhile, ConsenSys has expanded to a thousand employees, building critical infrastructure for the Ethereum (ETH) ecosystem to increase the value of the ETH it holds.

Payment tokens

With the emergence of the token sale, a new generation of blockchain projects has formed their business models around payment tokens inside networks, building two-sided markets and requiring the use of a native token for all transactions. According to the assumptions, demand for the limited native payment token will increase as the network's economy expands, resulting in a rise in the token's value.

Burn tokens

Corporations and projects that use a token to establish communities may not always transfer earnings to token holders directly. Buybacks/token burns, for example, have attracted a lot of attention as one of the features of the Binance (BNB) and MakerDAO (MKR) tokens. As revenue flows into the project (via MakerDAO stability fees and Binance trading fees), native tokens are repurchased from the public market and burnt, resulting in a reduction in the number of tokens and a price increase.

Taxation on speculation

The next wave of business models focused on developing the financial infrastructure for these native assets, including custodians, exchanges, and derivatives providers. They were all built with the same purpose in mind: to give services to people interested in speculating on these high-risk assets. Organizations like Coinbase can't lock in a monopolistic position by giving "exclusive access" because the underlying networks are open and permissionless. Nevertheless, such organizations' liquidity and branding generate defensible moats over time.

What distinguishes Web 3.0 from its predecessors?

User data will no longer be managed as intermediaries are no longer engaged in Web 3.0. This reduces the chances of censorship by the government or corporations and the efficacy of denial-of-service (DoS) attacks.

As more goods become linked to the internet, larger databases provide more information for computers to examine. This will enable them to provide more accurate information suited to each user's needs.

Finding the best-refined result on search engines was challenging before Web 3.0. Over time, though, they have increased their capacity to find semantically relevant results depending on search context and information. As a result, online surfing becomes easier, enabling everyone to get the information they seek quickly.

Customer service is important for a great user experience on online apps and websites. However, many successful online companies are unable to extend their customer care operations due to excessive costs. Users can have a better experience interacting with support professionals by deploying intelligent chatbots that can converse with several customers simultaneously, thanks to Web 3.0.

CHAPTER 7
AUGMENTED REALITY (AR)

A R is a digitally enhanced version of the real world generated via the use of digital visual elements, sound, or other sensory stimulation. It's becoming more popular among companies that deal with mobile computing and commercial apps.

As data collection and analysis expands, one of the main goals of augmented reality is to highlight particular aspects of the physical environment, increase understanding of those qualities, and provide useful and accessible information that can be utilized in real-world applications. Such b Big data can help organizations make better decisions and acquire insight into customer purchasing habits, among other things.

Augmented reality (AR) is a technique for enhancing one's experience by overlaying visual, audio, or other sensory information onto the real world.

Retailers and other businesses can utilize augmented reality to sell products and services, conduct innovative marketing campaigns, and gather unique user data.

Unlike virtual reality, which creates its virtual world, augmented reality enhances the present.

Augmented reality is evolving and becoming widely used in various applications. Since its inception, marketers, and technology companies have struggled to fight the impression that augmented reality is nothing more than a marketing tool. On the other hand, consumers appear to be reaping concrete benefits from this feature and anticipate it as part of their buying process.

For instance, some early adopters in the retail sector have created technology to improve the shopping experience for customers. Stores can let customers see how different goods might look in different contexts by introducing augmented reality into catalog applications. When shopping for furniture, customers point the camera in the direction of the desired room, and the object appears in the front.

Aside from that, the benefits of augmented reality might extend to the healthcare industry, where it could play a far larger role. One way is to employ applications that allow users to examine extremely detailed, 3D images of various bodily systems by hovering their mobile device over the target image. For instance, for medical practitioners, augmented reality might be a useful learning tool throughout their training.

According to some experts, Wearable devices might be a game-changer for augmented reality. Smart eyewear, for instance, may enable a more complete link between the actual and virtual domains if it improves sufficiently to become mainstream, whereas smartphones and tablets only show a small fraction of the user's landscape.

Virtual Reality vs. Augmented Reality

To improve the experience, augmented reality leverages the current real-world environment and overlays virtual information on top of it.

On the other hand, virtual reality immerses users, allowing them to "inhabit" a completely new environment, namely one developed and rendered by computers. Users may be submerged in an animated scene or a photograph of a real-world site that has been integrated into a virtual reality program. Users can look up, down, or any other direction using a virtual reality viewer as if they were truly there.

CHAPTER 8

NTF'S AND METAVERSE

T he goal of technology is to address real-life problems and blur the gap between reality and the virtual world. Every technology evolves throughout time for this to be achievable. As a result of these internet iterations, new tech trends like web 3 and Metaverse have emerged. On the other hand, these technologies take advantage of blockchain and its well-known use cases, such as NFTs, to realize the full potential of their initiatives.

Let's talk about Metaverse because it's all the rage right now. Although many tech futurists define Metaverse differently, the essential notion is that it aims to redefine our digital experiences. It's important to remember that Metaverse can be both centralized and decentralized. The notion of Facebook's Metaverse and other internet giants' is more of a centralized virtual world in which Facebook's CEO has ultimate control over or management of everything in their Metaverse.

Because the future is decentralized, our focus in this insight is on blockchain-powered Metaverse. Furthermore, we will address the function of NFTs in the Metaverse's virtual space. We'll find persuasive solutions to the queries, "How do NFTs connect to the Metaverse?" and "How do NFTs link to the Metaverse?"

Metaverse is a 3D virtual environment that combines our social and real-life lives to create an interesting digital experience. In 1992, Neal

Stephenson invented the word in his science fiction novel Snow Crash. The modern Metaverse is far from the original version and a fictional internet iteration governed by VR and AR technology.

What are NFTs in the Metaverse?

Non-fungible tokens (NFTs) indicate a person's ownership of digital assets such as digital art, paintings, social media posts, signatures, and so on. NFT can represent the tokenized form of real-world assets, such as land and buildings, in addition to intangible or digital material.

Non-fungible tokens (NFTs) and the technology that supports them are critical to the Metaverse's development. NFTs exist on the blockchain, which was first used to exchange digital assets but now have many applications. When we show the role of NFTs in the Metaverse's digital environment, we can see how they connect with existing VR and AR technologies to manage the whole space.

It implies that NFTs may represent ownership of everything in the Metaverse, including virtual avatars, real estate holdings (digital version), and in-game assets. Similarly, the Metaverse-based NFT marketplace allows users' avatars to browse the marketplace, examine the digital items in greater detail, and select the product of their choice.

The Metaverse, like any other invention, is undergoing numerous tests, and many groups are trying to set up new initiatives using Metaverse's core technology. In this sense, let us look at the Metaverse and see how it affects the digital world.

How does NFT work in the Metaverse?

NFTs function in the Metaverse the same way real-world objects do in the actual world. Simply defined, NFTs are a critical component of the emergent Metaverse, whose survival is dependent on asset tokenization.

To make use of the combined benefits of NFTs and Metaverse, any Metaverse endeavor, whether gaming or business, must mix the two. Some computer experts believe Metaverse and NFTs are mutually beneficial. In the Metaverse, NFTs are useful in a variety of ways. NFTs play an important role in providing asset ownership to enable interoperable blockchain games.

NFT technology is required to provide the asset owner with real digital ownership. However, the feasibility of NFTs in blockchain games is the primary reason for their popularity in the Metaverse. Interoperable games stimulate the development of gaming Metaverses by complementing the virtual environment. NFTs play the following roles in the Metaverse:

Through NFTs, Metaverse gives users access to their digital avatars (replicas of real-life identities). Every avatar is tokenized to establish ownership of the character.

NFT ticketing system distributes tickets to the intended audiences at Metaverse events such as live events and music concerts.

The NFT system is used to grant ownership and transfer it for trade in the secondary market for in-game goods and accessories like skins, tanks, and armors.

What role do NFTs play in the Metaverse's future?

NFTs can potentially change the way people engage with standard social media platforms and socialize. Let's see how NFTs can disrupt the current digital world: -

A fair and transparent economy

The Metaverse's decentralized virtual realm allows corporations and people to replicate and transfer real-world assets. Play-to-earn games are a popular way to integrate additional digital items into the Metaverse. Such games increase player engagement and empower them by giving perks such as in-game financing and trading.

Players can use NFTs to engage in play-to-earn games and earn money for their contributions. These games have guilds acting as middlemen to buy gaming assets, land, collectibles, and other real estates. Guilds are also responsible for paying players who have run out of capital.

This promotes a transparent and fair economy since anybody can join play-to-earn games and earn yield even if they have no capital to start with.

Next-generation of social experiences

NFTs play a critical role in the Metaverse, which redefines current social experiences. Users can confirm their identity among the different avatars accessible in the virtual realm by using their unique NFT avatars. Brands can utilize their NFT avatars to communicate with specific audiences, exchange project views with like-minded individuals, and solve various challenges.

Instead of a text-based conversation or video call, social media users can meet the avatar of their connection or social media buddy thanks to NFT avatars. Because NFTs have non-fungible properties, each NFT avatar is distinct and has a distinct identity in the actual world. Additionally, users in the Metaverse have total control over the design and curation of their unique virtual avatars.

Virtual real estate trends

In the Metaverse, users can acquire virtual properties just like they do in the real world. Users can own and create virtual real estate depending on their preferences, thanks to the underlying blockchain technology and NFTs. Users can purchase and sell virtual properties and rent them out for passive revenue.

Furthermore, people can build various structures on the virtual land, such as online stores, and use these places to host social gatherings. One of the greatest realistic examples of how virtual items are auctioned in NFTs is Decentraland. Many sectors have been drawn to the concept of virtual real estate because it allows for the online sale of tickets and merchandise.

How can businesses leverage NFTs in the Metaverse?

Businesses can use NFTs in a variety of ways. Physical bounds no longer restrict them because Metaverse provides them with a virtual environment that addresses the constraints of the actual world. The top three ways that NFTs may help enterprises are listed below.

Virtual product trading

The Metaverse is dominated by NFT trading. This virtual product can be a digital replica of a real product or a unique virtual product, such as tweets and png photos. Although these things do not exist in the actual world, people spend a lot of money on them.

People who own virtual products in the Metaverse enjoy similar benefits to those who buy them in real life. It's not surprising, for example, to see someone spend thousands of dollars to win a race in a high-end racing car. Not only do avatars in the Metaverse purchase and sell assets using NFTs, but they also debate transactions with one another. As a result, NFTs are an important part of the Metaverse's trading and exchange activity.

Reaching Worldwide audience

Few brands could foresee the enormous advantage of NFTs long before they became widespread, and they began using NFT technology to improve their brand. Companies worldwide are leveraging virtual products and NFTs to reach a larger audience.

The gaming sector was one of the first to implement NFT technology, and it has greater potential to draw younger viewers than any blockbuster film or sporting event. Even well-known businesses now offer the digital version of their goods before the physical version is released. NFTs help companies build popularity and effectively engage potential customers in this way.

Easy transfer of ownership

With numerous real-world use cases across various sectors, NFT has progressed significantly. They're no longer merely for buying and selling digital assets; luxury fashion businesses have begun distributing relevant NFTs to promote their products and services.

Brands launch their NFTs, and people invest in them, which is exactly what happens in the Metaverse. The transfer of ownership is also managed by NFT technology, ensuring that immutability is maintained. NFTs provide a simple way to exchange gaming collectibles while maintaining original ownership in the gaming industry.

Maintaining digital scarcity

Counterfeiting is a major issue in a variety of businesses. Even huge businesses battle to keep their products' value, knowing they might be counterfeited and sold for less money. Product features and design differences distinguish duplicates from originals in the actual world, but how can scarcity be maintained in the virtual world? That's when NFTs come in handy.

NFTs are based on blockchain and its non-fungible characteristics, which provide immutability in records and unique ownership features. Even if virtual items are easy to replicate, once tokenized using NFT, products, whether avatars or digital assets, cannot be replicated. It's difficult to survive in the Metaverse without digital scarcity, as anyone can counterfeit things and disrupt the entire system.

CHAPTER 9

HOW TO CREATE, BUY AND SELL NFTS

NFTs have become one of the most popular crypto trends in 2021, with global sales up 55 percent from $250 million to $389 million since 2020. Here's how to create, buy, and sell these well-known digital assets.

Since the introduction of Bitcoin Colored Coins in 2012, non-fungible tokens (NFTs) have thrived as unique collectible crypto assets. These coins were just *satoshis*, which are minuscule fractions of a bitcoin, with unique data that could be used to link them to real-world assets, such as "this satoshi represents $500 of John Doe's New York office building." Colored Coins were mostly used to create and trade artwork on Counterparty, a peer-to-peer trading network built on Bitcoin's blockchain, such as "Rare Pepe" digital cards.

These cartoon frog drawings based on a widespread internet fad were among the first examples of distinctive digital artwork tied to crypto coins. This paved the door for new non-fungible token standards — a collection of blockchain building blocks that allow developers to create their NFTs — to be conceived and developed.

NFTs can be used to represent almost any intangible or tangible object, such as:

• Artwork

• Music

• Virtual items within video games such as virtual currency, skins, avatars, and weapons

• Collectibles (e.g., digital trading cards)

• Video footage of iconic sporting moments

• Virtual land

• Tokenized real-world assets, from real estate and cars to designer sneakers and racehorses.

How to create NFTs

Creating your own NFT artwork, whether in the form of a GIF or an image, is a rather simple process that does not require extensive crypto expertise. NFT Artwork can be used to create collectibles such as digital card sets.

You must first decide which blockchain you want to use to issue your NFTs. The most widely used blockchain platform for issuing NFTs is Ethereum. Several alternative blockchains, however, are gaining traction, including:

- Flow by Dapper Labs

- Binance Smart Chain

- Cosmos

- WAX

- Polkadot

- Tron

- EOS

- Tezos

Each blockchain has its unique NFT token standard, marketplaces, and compatible wallet services. If you create NFTs on the Binance Smart Chain, you can only sell them on sites that accept Binance Smart Chain assets. This means you would not be able to sell them on a marketplace like VIV3, built on the Flow blockchain, or OpenSea, which is based on the Ethereum blockchain.

Because Ethereum has the largest NFT ecosystem, you will need the following to mint your NFT video, music, or artwork on the Ethereum blockchain:

- An Ethereum wallet, such as Trust Wallet, Coinbase Wallet, or MetaMask, supports ERC-721

• In ether, you'll need about $50-$100. (ETH). You can buy ether with British pounds sterling, US dollars, and other fiat currencies if you use Coinbase's wallet. Otherwise, you'll have to buy ether from a cryptocurrency exchange.

Once you have these, you can link your wallet to several NFT-centric services and upload the image or file you wish to make into an NFT.

The most popular Ethereum NFT exchanges are:

• OpenSea

• Mintable

• Rarible

Rarible, Mintable, and OpenSea have a "create" button in the top right corner.

This is how it works on OpenSea, the world's largest Ethereum-based NFT marketplace.

When you click the blue "Create" button, you'll be taken to a screen where you'll be asked to connect your Ethereum wallet. Once you have entered your wallet password when requested, it'll automatically connect your wallet with the marketplace. To confirm you hold the wallet address, you may need to sign a message in your Ethereum wallet digitally, but it's only a matter of clicking through.

There is no fee for digitally signing a message; it is simply a way to show that you control the wallet.

The next step on OpenSea is to select "my collections" by hovering over "create" in the top right corner. Then, as shown below, click the blue "create" button.

Creating an NFT collection on OpenSea

You will be shown a window where you can upload your artwork, give it a name, and add a description.

This part is just you creating a folder for your newly created NFTs to go   in.

OpenSea NFT collection creation window

Once you have assigned an image to your collection, it will appear as seen below. After that, click the pencil symbol in the top right corner to add a banner image to the page.

Add a banner image to NFT collection on OpenSea

Your page should end up appearing similar to the one below.

You are now ready to create your first NFT. Sign another message by clicking the "Add New Item" button on your wallet.

Creating NFT collection on OpenSea

You can upload your NFT music, image, 3D model, or GIF in a new window.

You can also include specific attributes and traits to boost the uniqueness and scarcity of your NFT on OpenSea and other marketplaces. Creators can incorporate unlockable content that can only be accessed by the purchaser. This can be passwords, discount codes, certain services, and contact information.

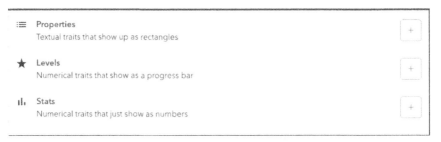

NFT traits on the Ethereum-based OpenSea platform.

When you're finished, click "create" at the bottom of the screen and confirm the NFT's creation by signing another message in your wallet. After that, you should add the artwork to your collection.

What does it cost to create NFTs?

While creating NFTs on OpenSea is free, there are fees on other sites. On Ethereum-based networks, this fee is referred to as "gas." The amount of ether required to do a certain activity on the blockchain – in this case, adding a new NFT to the marketplace – is known as Ethereum gas. The cost of gas varies depending on network congestion. Gas prices rise in direct proportion to the number of users trading value over the network at any one time, and vice versa.

Top tip: Ethereum gas fees are much lower on weekends, when fewer people trade value across the network. If you're selling a lot of NFTs, this can help you save money.

How to sell NFTs

Find your NFTs in your collection, click, and then check for the "sell" button on a marketplace. By choosing this option, you'll be led to a pricing page where you may set the sale's terms, such as whether to sell at a fixed price or have an auction.

Ether and other ERC-20 tokens are the most common cryptocurrencies for which you can sell your NFTs; however, some platforms only accept the native currency of the blockchain they were built on. VIV3, for instance, is a Flow blockchain marketplace that solely accepts FLOW tokens.

You can program in royalties and choose which ERC-20 token you'd like to obtain for selling the NFT by hitting the "edit" button next to the collection image on OpenSea, signing the message with your wallet, and scrolling down. NFT creators can earn a commission every time the item is sold to a new person, thanks to royalties. For artists and other content creators, smart contracts can automatically provide an infinite supply of passive income.

Selling NFTs on OpenSea

A fee is sometimes required to complete the process of listing NFTs on a marketplace. While this is not true for every platform, it is something to consider when creating NFTs.

How to Buy NFTs

Before you purchase NFTs, there are 4 things you should think about:

• What marketplace do you plan on purchasing the NFTs from?

• What wallet should you download to connect with the platform and buy NFTs?

• Which cryptocurrency do you need to fund the wallet with to execute the transaction?

• Will the NFTs you want to buy be available at a specific time, i.e., through an art drop or a pack?

Some NFTs are only available on specific platforms. For instance, to buy NBA Top Shot packs, you will need to register with NBA Top Shot, create a Dapper wallet, and fund it with either the USDC stable coin or supporting fiat money. You'll also have to wait for one of the card pack drops to be announced and hope that you can get one before they sell out.

CHAPTER 10
TIPS & SECRETS TO GET HUGE PROFIT FROM NFT INVESTING

Many NFT creators, artists, and collectors are now clamoring to participate in this burgeoning trend. However, is there a lot of profit to be made from NFTs? In fact, how do you earn a profit on non-fungible token purchases? So, after doing a lot of research on this topic, here's what I discovered.

You can profit from your NFT purchase in several ways:

1. Flip Your NFT (Buy NFTs, then swiftly resell them for a profit.)
2. Your NFT can be sold (When there is a sudden spike or steady climb in recent sales.)
3. Hold Onto Your NFT (If your NFT has underlying value, it'll likely rise in value over time.)
4. Unlockables (This is exclusives available to the NFT owner.)
5. Purchase what you believe in (Buying an NFT you believe in can result in better-educated purchases.)

Now, let's take a closer look at the many ways to profit from your NFT purchases.

Flip Your NFT

Flipping an NFT is one of the most typical ways to profit from purchase. To flip your NFT, simply buy one and immediately put it back on the market for a higher price. The best part of flipping a non-fungible token vs a traditional item like a house is that it doesn't require remodeling or updating. It's as simple as buying it and then selling it.

If you want to have the highest chance of flipping your NFT, look for one that has a constant upward sales trend. Furthermore, if you have the opportunity to purchase a low-cost NFT from a well-known developer, you may be able to immediately sell it for a huge return on investment (ROI).

Resell Your NFT

Rather than purchasing and immediately flipping your non-fungible token, you can buy one and hold onto it for a while until you witness a drastic increase in sales/sale prices or a constant and consistent growth over time. The secret to successfully reselling your NFT is to not keep it for too long.

It may be a good idea to sell your NFT shortly following a steady increase in sale prices or a sudden rise. If you wait too long, you might not make any money or possibly lose money. Remember that you must ride the wave, but every wave will eventually come to an end.

Hold Onto Your NFT

If you are in the NFT space for a long time and not simply looking to make a quick profit, investing in a long-term NFT could be a good idea. If you can find an NFT with underlying value for a low price now, it could be worth a fortune in the future. The most important aspect of this strategy is to ensure that the non-fungible token you buy has real value and is not just a quick fad.

Anything considered valuable, exclusive, or unique could be a smart long-term investment.

Unlockables

NFT Assets that are held on a decentralized storage network are known as unlockables. When someone buys a non-fungible token with these unlockables, they gain access to a variety of benefits, including:

- Merch Deals
- VIP access to live shows
- Monthly Meetings
- Exclusive Calls
- Physical Product
- Follows on social media

When it comes to NFT unlockables, the options are unlimited. I recommend purchasing NFTs with valuable unlockables if you can. You can take advantage of all the perks even if you don't resell it!

Buy What You Believe In

It's important to purchase an NFT that you're passionate about. In general, if you are interested in a subject, you will better understand that subject. This means you have a better chance of buying something profitable because you know better.

It's just the right thing to do. You may either jump on the bandwagon and start buying trendy items you know nothing about, or you can make a more informed decision and support someone who makes something you truly enjoy. It's entirely up to you, but I only purchase items that I like.

Overall, if your primary goal is to profit from NFTs, you must research to guarantee that you purchase an NFT that will deliver a return on investment.

NFT Categories with High Potential Profit

There are many different kinds of non-fungible tokens to choose from, and the list will only get longer. Here are some of the most popular NFT categories available to purchase and profit from:

- Art
- Music
- Gaming
- Photography

Art

Thousands of digital art NFTs are available for purchase. Look for one that has the potential to be valuable in the future. Also, anything you think would make wonderful memorabilia.

Digital art is fantastic because you can create it and transfer it to someone else right away. It is now possible to purchase a portion of digital artwork. That's exactly what the $69 million buyers of Beelple's piece did. He sold shares of the piece to multiple people.

The good news is that if you are a creator, you can not only sell your work, but you can also set up NFTs so that you automatically receive a percentage of all secondary sales, which is known as royalty. Previously, as an artist, you could not receive any proceeds from secondary sales in the art world, but that is no longer the case.

NFTs can be utilized to make programmable art as well. Programmable art refers to artwork programmed to exhibit dynamic qualities based on how the code is implemented on the blockchain. A digital marketplace called ASYNC art is one place where you can make programmable art. You can not only make your master copy there, but you can also add individual layers and change their attributes.

Individuals can contribute to the art as a group, and different group members can control their activities. As a result, NFTs allow for collective art. Your art can be displayed on online marketplaces such as

SuperRare and OpenSea, where it can be bought and sold once it has been created.

Music

NFTs have enormous potential in the music industry! You can get lifetime VIP access to events, meetings, phone conversations, and more, but that's just the beginning. Consider this: music artists can suddenly use non-fungible tokens to fund their careers. This means that record label deals may no longer be necessary for musicians, and the artist may keep a larger portion of the profit for themselves.

Furthermore, NFTs allow the artist and the audience to connect on a much deeper level than before. When it comes to minting tokens, musicians have so many customizable possibilities to include anything they want.

Gaming

With the purchase and sale of in-game items, money is made on popular video game platforms. Games like Dota 2 and Team Fortress 2 on the Steam marketplace, for example, are extremely popular and sell quickly.

Crypto Kitties is another NFT phenomenon. Crypto Kitties are being purchased and bred to sell them. Another attractive niche to profit from is in-game items.

Furthermore, because it is decentralized, there is no limit to the types of game items that can be sold or the amounts that can be sold. Axie Infinity, one of the most popular games, has seen some high-ticket purchases. Other games, such as Skyview, Gods of Change, and others, can be swapped or sold for other cards.

Photography

Kate Woodman recently received $20,000 for a single NFT photograph. Photographs are ideal for NFTs because they are now digital.

Photographs capture moments, and some of these moments are significant to people. You can buy images or make your own NFTs and sell them on the various marketplaces.

The best part is that you don't have to give up your copyright or reproduction rights as a photographer. You are just selling the buyer the ownership of the NFT piece. You can keep showing that image or photograph, sell prints, or license it to companies.

Once you've determined whether you'll buy or create NFTs, you'll need to decide which type of NFTs you'll use. The next stage is to put them on the marketplaces for sale.

Best Tip to Sell Your NFTs For Profit.

Determine Which Marketplace you want to sell on

If you have NFTs that you purchased and want to sell, you can do so directly on the marketplaces. However, you should inquire about the fees that will be charged. You can go to prominent market spaces like OpenSea, SuperRare, and Nifty Gateway once you have the digital asset you wish to sell.

You have complete control over the number of editions you wish to sell. It does not have to be only one edition. You can have multiple editions of the same digital asset, and each will be distinct and have its token id. Please keep in mind, though, that having more can potentially lower the value of your asset.

Once you've done this, your digital item can't be duplicated or replaced in any way. As a result, no unique abilities or talents are required. You can benefit from locating or constructing an NFT that appeals to people in a specific niche.

Set a reserve bid, which is the lowest price you're willing to sell it for. This is similar to auction websites such as eBay. Don't overprice it or underprice it. Look for a reasonable profit margin, and it will sell.

Finding solid digital assets that have underlying value or that you believe will have value in the future is one method to profit from NFT. Invest in NFTs that you are confident will yield a profit when sold. Once you've purchased these, you can resell them on a marketplace for a considerably higher price. You can also utilize a variety of advertising methods to increase bids.

The value of NFTs is determined by two factors: novelty and scarcity. Focusing on these two aspects can result in a high amount of value for your digital content. One of the secrets to profiting is acquiring appealing and unique creative art, music, and collectibles. It is vital to know the fees and transactions to avoid losing money on your transactions.

CHAPTER 11

MARKETING IN THE AGE OF THE METAVERSE

The Metaverse is read, and it's time to adapt marketing methods to a new digital reality.

If you're new to the Metaverse, you've been living under a rock and need to catch up on where the world is going – the entire world, not just the marketing world. If you've already heard about it, brace yourself: the future is here, and you must start planning for it right now.

In many aspects, the term "metaverse" is similar to "internet." It's one of those digital buzzwords that's sticking around — and it's changing the way people operate. That's why, just as the Internet opened new opportunities for brand promotion and growth in the digital world, it's equally critical from a marketing standpoint to grasp what changes the Metaverse will bring.

As already mentioned, Neal Stephenson initially mentioned the concept of a Metaverse in his novel Snow Crash, published in 1992. It was then used as the inspiration for the Oasis in Ernest Cline's novel Ready Player One.

The concept of the Metaverse reappeared nearly three decades later in an essay by venture investor Matthew Ball, who outlined a textbook description and features of the Metaverse. It features a fully functioning, autonomous economy. It is characterized by a concept called "interoperability," which means that all things and avatars within the Metaverse can be transported from one section of the Metaverse to another, irrespective of whose jurisdiction they fall under.

The Metaverse is basically what the internet will develop into as the world grows more digital by the day, bringing all of the above together. The term "metaverse" currently refers to a reality that extends beyond the physical and into the digital, with experiences and values that exist in both realms at the same time.

What does this imply in terms of marketing? The Metaverse presents a whole new arena for companies to have a strong presence and engage with customers, so it's both an opportunity and a difficulty. It is, however, unknown ground that demands strategic planning to enable a seamless but memorable introduction into a whole new universe that is consistent with (and compliments) your brand identity.

Why now?

It takes the right mix of a strong concept, the right timing, and the appropriate context for certain digital trends to take root and upend the world as we know it. All three aspects came together in the Metaverse to create a fortunate environment where the idea could permeate people's lives and possibly dictate the future.

Then there's the issue of timing. The COVID-19 epidemic boosted global digital change considerably. Life on digital platforms became the new normal overnight. Work became more flexible, online entertainment got more popular, and new venues for communication, education, entertainment, and services arose — and the world as we knew it was forever changed.

The way companies thought about marketing and advertising altered due to this fundamental shift in customer behavior. Instead of focusing on reallocating media budgets from channel to channel or media placements, the marketing strategy's fundamental focus shifted to narrative, brand equity, customer experience, and consumer interaction. Suddenly, success was no longer dependent on strategic budget allocation. Instead, marketers sought to develop a sense of belonging in their customers who had spent almost a year in quarantine through meaningful experiences, consistency, authenticity, and a sense of belonging.

Second, there's the broader background of technology breakthroughs that are driving the digital transition. Virtual reality (VR) and augmented reality (AR), for example, have surged in popularity and use during the last four years. In 2018, 59.5 million people in the United States utilized augmented reality at least once a month, according to Statista. According to projections, by 2022, this number will have surpassed 95 million users.

Number of augmented reality (AR) and virtual reality (VR) users in the U.S. from 2017 to 2022

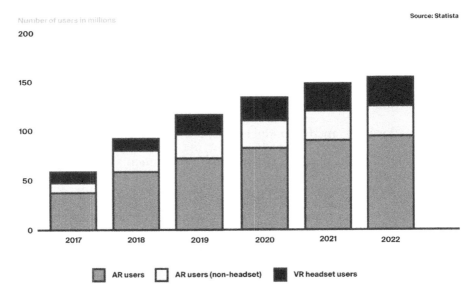

Number of virtual reality (VR) and augmented reality (AR) users in the United States from 2017 to 2022

Number of users in millions

Source: Statista

AR users   AR users (non-headset)   VR headset users

Many IT businesses are jumping on this trend, and as it gains traction (and alters things), the number of companies investing in the Metaverse is rapidly expanding.

Facebook has stated its desire to invest roughly $10 billion in Facebook Reality Labs, its AR and VR research organization, among other internet titans. With the formal announcement of the firm's renaming as Meta, it's evident that the corporation is well on its way to establishing its Metaverse. While Meta already has the gear to construct its digital

96

world (think Oculus and, more recently, the Ray-Ban smart glasses), it plans to create a completely new digital cosmos that these headsets can easily access. Like Google, Microsoft, and Amazon, other firms have expressed interest in expanding their AR/VR investments and entering the Metaverse.

As a marketer, it's vital to remain current with new technology and assess how it will impact its market position. VR/AR is just the beginning of what the Metaverse offers in terms of immersion and interaction with loyal or potential consumers. New technologies bring new opportunities for engagement, activations, and placements.

It's worth noting that, for a long time, conventional marketing thought of brand values and messaging as an unchanging basis, with technology being used to implement innovative strategies. Now, the picture has changed: technology has become the bedrock upon which a brand's narrative is built, allowing for wider reach, additional touchpoints, and more possibilities to interact with customers.

Groundbreaking. But is it?

Although the term "metaverse" sounds far-fetched, it is more realistic than you would believe.

The fact is that the Metaverse's hints have been around for quite some time, even if they were not as evident as one might think. To become a pioneer, trailblazer, and expert in the field, you must first grasp and apply the Metaverse to your marketing strategies.

Popular video gaming platforms like Roblox and Fortnite are prime instances of the Metaverse present in our daily lives. These games allow players to construct their worlds, and that ability is no longer confined to individual players. It has also been extended to brands and businesses to develop a significant presence in this new digital world.

According to the New York Times, gamers spent around 10 billion hours on Roblox in early 2021, and more than 42 million people logged into the gaming site daily. Players have spent $652 million on digital things for their avatars in the games' economy, based on its currency, known as Robux.

Both Roblox and Fortnite have evolved into more than just game platforms. They sprang from the gaming industry by hosting large-scale events such as concerts and shows that brought people together for a shared digital experience. In 2020, Lil Nas X, for instance, staged a virtual concert on Roblox that garnered over 30 million visitors over four days. Ariana Grande used Fortnite to present her brand-new Rift Tour concert event.

Any other video game or social networking platform that allows players to create their avatars and appear via them is closer to becoming "metaversal" than you would believe.

The distinction between traditional reality and virtual reality is no longer discernible. It's past time to figure out what it means and how we can be ready for the new world we're about to enter.

Entering the Metaverse as a Marketer

To say that the Metaverse will revolutionize marketing as we know it is an understatement. Many technologies have revolutionized marketing and advertising, ranging from new platforms to artificial intelligence. The Metaverse, on the other hand, offers up a whole new world of endless possibilities, and it's up to us to face the unknown and learn to adapt through quick experimentation and risk-taking.

The emergence of the Metaverse suggests a shift away from traditional marketing and toward creating genuine, engaging brand experiences that develop strong customer connections. Building relationships, accessing existing communities, and forming new ones would precedence over "growth hacking," which was the standard for unlocking efficiency through quick optimizations.

Marketing in the Metaverse will be centered on the user's experience and directed by the community. It will be important to question why you believe customers want to interact with your business on a strategic level. Are you having enough fun and excitement with your experiences? Is it possible to relate to them? Do they provide an immersive experience? Finally, do they have any significance? These are the questions you should be considering when you begin your journey through the Metaverse.

In the Metaverse, the term "community" should always be remembered. In this new reality, brands may expand and scale by establishing their worlds and meaningfully engaging with (and contributing to) established and powerful communities in the digital realm.

Ownership, Belonging, and NFTs

NFT has become one of the trendiest buzzwords in the tech sector over the last year. Non-fungible tokens, or NFTs, are digital assets comparable to bitcoin, except that they are unique and cannot be replaced or replicated. Possessing an NFT is the digital equivalent of owning a rare art or original work in the real world. NFTs can take several forms, ranging from a monetary investment to a digitally worn item.

To date, the most prevalent NFTs have been working by digital artists or well-known artists that make digital-first representations of their work that are intended for digital distribution. However, brands and industries increasingly see the NFT space (and, by extension, the Metaverse) as a unique growth opportunity. Several have already initiated digital drops and releases to establish themselves in the digital world.

Hollywood and the fashion business are also examples of NFT projects. The following are just a handful of the many NFT releases that have occurred in less than a year:

Quentin Tarantino has announced the release of extra content from his highly lauded film Pulp Fiction.

In early 2021, Marvel released NFTs in preparation for the new Spider-Man film release.

NFL fans can purchase virtual commemorative tickets as NFTs from Thanksgiving through the end of 2021.

Simone Biles has teamed up with Autograph to release new NFTs 8-bit animations of some of her most famous Olympic performances.

The above is a tip of the iceberg, but one common thread runs through all of the above (and future) releases: When implemented effectively, NFTs can be a great strategic factor for brand success.

NFTs are important in the Metaverse because they a) provide customers a sense of ownership and belonging and b) allow marketers to take community-building to new heights.

Through digital collectibles, NFTs create various avenues for businesses to enhance their authority and tell their distinctive story. They allow for the creation of hype around specific events or product launches by allowing early access to tokens and fostering anticipation, similar to how "drops" are popular in the real world today. NFTs also provides a unique chance to add a digital asset to offline service, product, or experience. This allows companies to diversify their income streams while also multiplying the reach of a campaign.

Collectibles have long been used to create a culture of affinity. It is founded on the timeless principle of scarcity, which increases the value of a product or service. Collecting rare branded products, such as shoes, magazine editions, and toys. The problem has always been to digitally reproduce this model.

NFTs have finally made the unthinkable feasible by introducing an experience that can validate digital valuables and is based on authenticity, trust, and, of course, affinity. Furthermore, when NFTs are linked to real-world offline services, they create new opportunities for engaging, thrilling, and immersive experiences that foster a stronger bond with customers.

The Metaverse, like AR and VR, isn't immune to this tendency. A strong brand that pulls people together and generates meaningful experiences is necessary for survival and future success in this new environment.

Brands Charting the Path in the Metaverse

Some businesses have established their own branded worlds to encourage a feeling of belonging and excitement in the virtual community, whether via experiences or digital collectibles. Developers and gamers may construct their worlds in the Metaverse.

It's just as vital to participating with communities in meaningful and thoughtful ways as it is to create your community and virtual world. This entails maintaining a constant eye on community member trends and responding to them at the right time, with the proper plan.

Let's look at some of the greatest examples of brands putting community first in their meta-campaigns and initiatives.

Gucci

Gucci was one of the first premium brands to release unique NFTs. The fashion brand staged an online auction of an NFT film called Aria, which was inspired by its Fall/Winter 2021 collection in partnership with Christie's. In June 2021, it was sold for $25,000.

Gucci Garden on Roblox, an immersive virtual exhibit inspired by the Gucci Garden Archetypes, a multi-sensory experience in Florence, Italy, debuted in Spring 2021.

The virtual exhibit featured a randomized succession of themed rooms inspired by the brand's historical campaigns, design history, and prior muses and was open for two weeks. As viewers progressed through the experience, their avatars changed, taking on new colors, patterns, and other effects. RookVanguard built a store with limited-edition virtual Gucci products for sale during the exhibit.

Gucci, a premium brand that is often seen as out of reach, used the Metaverse to create a more community-centric environment that created a new way for customers worldwide to engage with the brand. The concepts of interacting and cultivating a sense of belonging within the virtual community underpin the virtual experience — and the world Gucci developed.

Nike

Nike is another brand that is often at the forefront of innovation, so it's no surprise that the sportswear company has already established its own Roblox Metaverse environment.

NIKELAND, Nike's universe set against its worldwide headquarters in Roblox's immersive 3D area. The brand's mission is simple: "to turn sport and play into a lifestyle."

NIKELAND is a virtual space patterned like Nike's real-world headquarters that allows Roblox players to build mini-games with interactive sports materials or play games like Tag, Dodgeball, and The Floor is Lava with their friends.

However, the meta characteristic of NIKELAND is that it bridges the gap between the physical and virtual worlds: The activities in which participants engage are not solely virtual. They can even convert offline motions from wearable devices into virtual environments, such as jumps or sprints.

The Nike universe, of course, has its store, where gamers can outfit their avatars in new items as well as classics like the Nike Blazer and the Air Force.

NIKELAND is one of the most effective examples of a company creating its universe while engaging the customer in two worlds — physical and online — to date.

Coca-Cola

The Metaverse is especially valuable to legacy brands because it provides an entirely new approach to relaunching the brand in a digital environment, reviving customers' memories of its history and fundamental values while monetizing its current services.

And Coca-Cola has done precisely that.

The beverage giant brought the pixelated version of the company's famous 1956 vending machine. Instead of carrying Coke cans, the "Friendship Box" was created to seem like a "loot box" from a video game. A custom Coca-Cola bubble jacket built for the Decentraland 3D platform, a sound visualizer including identifiable audio clips as you pour or sip the drink, and a Coca-Cola Friendship Card with redesigned artwork from the 1940s were all included in the treasure box.

Oh, and the auction winner also received an actual cooler full of Coca-Cola. Talk about bridging the gap between the physical and virtual worlds.

The activation reiterates the brand's key principles and distinct personality in numerous ways. Coca-Cola's ethos has been about bringing people together and enjoying them. Hence, it's only right that their first NFT, introduced on International Friendship Day, is a 'Surprise and Delight' friendship box.

What's even better? The digital memorabilia can be experienced again and over again because of its interactivity.

Balenciaga

Balenciaga is another luxury brand collaborating with Epic Games, the creators of Fortnite, to explore new territory in the Metaverse.

The partnership, which began in September 2021, will bring the game's premium fashion house's trademark designs. The total experience covers both the real and digital worlds, including in-game and offline clothes. Balenciaga clothing from earlier seasons may be used to dress up some of the game's prominent characters (from hoodies to sunglasses to boots). It's worth noting that Epic Games' collaboration with Balenciaga marks the company's first foray into the world of fashion and luxury.

The partnership comprised four virtual outfits (or "skins") for players to purchase, as well as additional products like accessories, weaponry, and even a virtual Balenciaga destination in-game (complete with a Balenciaga store). Limited-edition Balenciaga x Fortnite caps, hoodies, and t-shirts, all available on Balenciaga.com, were part of the offline activity.

Balenciaga revealed their Fall 2021 collection in the guise of its own game, Afterworld: the Age of Tomorrow, in December 2020. Players are transported in a dismal, futuristic environment and pass avatars clad in ripped jeans and armor-like boots from the brand's collection.

Balenciaga was one of the first fashion houses to integrate into the Fortnite community, creating a universe where gamers can utilize Balenciaga's design elements to build their designs and dress their avatars.

NASCAR

The business has now released a new digital race car that goes to the virtual streets of Jailbreak, a popular Roblox virtual reality game. NASCAR has not only perfectly incorporated itself into the Jailbreak environment with a virtual representation of its cars, but it has also taken the first steps toward community building by providing digital gear for users' avatars. The company even went so far as to allow players to create their custom uniforms and used the game's developers as social media influencers to promote the brand.

Is it possible to immerse yourself in the experience? Yes. Is NASCAR allowing users to form personal and deep connections with the brand, making them feel like they are part of a community? Yes. One of the first instances of a brand-forward and community-driven approach is NASCAR's program.

Chipotle

Luxury brands aren't the only ones making their first step into the metaverse. Some of the more well-known restaurant businesses are considering it, with Chipotle taking steps to make it a reality.

Chipotle announced in October 2021 that it would launch the first-ever virtual restaurant on Roblox to commemorate 21 years of Boorito, a famous Halloween event. Since 2000, Boorito has brought Chipotle customers together in costume for Halloween at various restaurant locations.

Chipotle's digital experience this year allowed visitors to virtually visit the restaurant for a chance to win a free burrito offer code, navigate the Chipotle Boorito Maze to find special virtual products, and even choose from various digital Chipotle-inspired costumes for their restaurant visit.

The Matrix, from Warner Bros., was one of the earliest depictions of a world where the real and the virtual merged. Warner Bros. has released 100,000 NFTs for fans of the franchise in 2021, coinciding with the new film's release. The NFTs depict the Matrix characters who live and breathe. Each NFT is worth $50 and allows the owner to pick between the red and blue pills, much as the characters in the films.

These NFTs exemplify the Metaverse's and crypto's potential. They launch a unique digital experience based on and inspired by a popular film franchise. Simultaneously, they present a whole new model for fan involvement and community development in online and real worlds. The interactive NFTs can be updated regularly, offering fans new options to connect with their favorite movies in both worlds.

This isn't the first time Warner Bros. has dabbled in the NFT and Metaverse. With the Space Jam series reboot in early 2021, the production firm launched the project with a free giveaway of NFTs to Space Jam enthusiasts.

Meta is the Way

The Metaverse isn't a myth or a work of fiction anymore. It's already here, and many businesses are eager to jump into the new digital world. As we live through 2022 and beyond, every brand must devise development plans that take advantage of the Metaverse's vast potential.

Brands must focus on developing experiences that create a community to succeed in a world where the barriers between the digital and real worlds are increasingly blurred. The ultimate objective is to connect customers on a new and deeper level and extend existing services to add NFTs that build anticipation and a sense of belonging.

The transition to a digital environment might be difficult to comprehend. By tapping into bringing more people into the digital space or virtual communities, you can construct new methods to build consumer relationships, establish a strong brand presence, and uncover new avenues for revenue.

CHAPTER 12

TOP METAVERSE STOCKS TO BUY IN 2022

Think long term. I'm aware that those three terms are often utilized. However, they aren't taken into account nearly enough. Keeping that in mind with the current stock market volatility is crucial.

Whatever the stock market does next week or next month, a few sectors should be enormous winners in the long run. I believe one of them is the metaverse. Here are five irresistible metaverse stocks to purchase in 2022 if you're a long-term investor.

1. Nvidia

Nvidia (NASDAQ: NVDA) is one of the best artificial intelligence (AI) stocks on the market. It's one of the market's finest gaming stocks. It's also a great metaverse stock right now and in the future.

While many companies are fighting for a piece of the metaverse pie, Nvidia has already released a successful product. The Omniverse technology, developed by the business, enables for virtual 3D design collaboration and simulation. Omniverse is utilized by various customers, including game developers, manufacturers, and engineering firms.

As the metaverse takes form, Nvidia's graphics processing units (GPUs) should be in great demand. Few companies can compete with Nvidia in terms of virtual reality app power.

2. Unity Software

This is a metaverse stock that I believe will quadruple in value by 2022. More than 70 percent of the top 1,000 mobile games have been created using its technologies. Unity believes that their platform will generate a similar amount of metaverse content.

However, the metaverse will not be built solely by programmers. Artists will also be significantly involved. Unity is now better positioned to meet client needs thanks to the purchase of Weta Digital.

You might not know what Weta is, but you've most definitely seen their work. The company's technology has been used to generate visual effects for several TV shows and movies, including The Lord of the Rings and Game of Thrones.

3. Meta Platforms

Meta Platforms (NASDAQ: FB) changed its name from Facebook because the metaverse is vital to its future. While advertising on its social networking applications covers the bills, for the time being, Meta is aggressively investing in the metaverse's development.

Mark Zuckerberg, the firm's CEO, has declared publicly that his company's objective is to help deliver the metaverse to at least one billion people. "This will enable a significantly greater creative economy of both digital and physical things," he believes.

Only a few companies can focus on the full metaverse ecosystem, including Meta. To make the metaverse a reality, it's working on an operating system, social network, e-commerce architecture, and augmented reality/virtual reality devices.

4. Adobe

Adobe (NASDAQ: ADBE) is a digital media giant. Although Adobe is well known for their Photoshop, Acrobat, and Creative Cloud products, it also has a fantastic tool called Aero that can be used to create augmented reality experiences.

"Adobe is the strongest software investment for the metaverse," according to Jefferies analyst Brent Thill. Shantanu Narayen, the CEO of Adobe, looks to be on the same page. In Adobe's fourth-quarter conference call in December, Narayen stated:

When I think of web 3D and the metaverse, what it truly means and suggests is that activities you're used to doing in the physical world will increasingly be done in the virtual world. So, whether you're buying, playing games, producing, co-creating with others, or expanding it, the idea of establishing all of that metaverse was, what better company on the earth than Adobe to be able to accomplish that?

You don't have to agree with Narayen or Thill to see Adobe's enormous potential in the metaverse.

5. Matterport

Smaller companies could potentially play an important part in the metaverse's growth. One such example is Matterport (NASDAQ: MTTR). The company's technology allows for developing "digital twins" of actual assets such as houses, offices, boats, and other structures.

The current market capitalization of Matterport is roughly $4 billion. On the other hand, the company is the 800-pound gorilla in the spatial data industry, which it was founded. On its platform, Matterport manages 6.2 million spaces, about 100 times the rest of the market combined.

However, the company has only taken a small portion of the $240 billion total addressable markets. Matterport appears to be on the verge of exploding in the future, thanks to the emergence of the metaverse.

CHAPTER 13

HOW METAVERSE IS EVOLVING DIGITAL WORLD

Outsiders often mix up Metaverse and Virtual Reality. They believe Metaverse is a new form of virtual reality technology. Some people believe it is the internet's future. Even if these notions are true, the digital world is evolving. Although it may appear to be science fiction, Metaverse digitally combines personal and business life in a similar way to our physical reality. However, you may be wondering why this technology is capturing people's interest and why they are investing so much in the digital world.

Unlike virtual reality (VR) technology, which we use in video games, Metaverse incorporates all potential activities. You can do everything online, from hanging out with pals to going to the movies, playing tennis, and going to concerts. Take a closer look at how Metaverse will transform our world:

1. Economic Changes

Metaverse will alter the way we do business in the future. It has an impact on how people think when they buy things. As a result, businesses will perform more market research to better understand their customers' behavior. The experience of buying things at a physical store is not the same as what Metaverse provides. So, every company must modernize its operations. Robots and virtual assistants will handle customer contacts. For data analysis, these bots will be equipped with sophisticated computer equipment.

2. Cultural Changes

Metaverse will affect cultural standards since it links people from many ethnic backgrounds. People in the Metaverse will have connections and friendships just like they do in the real world. They do, however, engage through holograms and self-contained NPCs. The Metaverse will impact the corporate world and will bring customers together in 3D. They won't be able to connect with marketing people, but they will speak with bots to get answers to their questions.

3. Shopping Experience

The Metaverse shopping experience is unique in comparison to physical purchasing. Virtual real estate, virtual fashion, and avatar skins have great value in the Metaverse. People will also invest in businesses and properties that do not exist physically. Because people will represent themselves with the avatar, the fashion industry will design clothing for the characters. People would also look for virtual designer clothes and houses to invest in.

4. Entertainment Industry

Virtual concerts, seminars, and gatherings will be customary in the Metaverse. Celebrities and companies will use the virtual world to interact with their fans. We now utilize technology to make purchases and play games. On the other hand, people would virtually spend time with their pals in restaurants, events, and cafés. Wendy's, for example, is experimenting with putting their restaurant in the Metaverse so that consumers may engage with their friends there. Ariana Grande's concert in Fortnite Metaverse on August 7, 2021, is another example of a Metaverse entertainment event.

Without question, the Metaverse will have massive implications in our society. It will alter the way we communicate, promote, and brand ourselves. In addition, this ground-breaking technology will present new opportunities and difficulties. The metaverse has the potential to unleash great creativity and expand our entertainment, economic, and cultural horizons.

CHAPTER 14

DECENTRALAND

Decentraland is an Ethereum-based program that aims to encourage a worldwide network of users to govern a shared virtual environment.

Users of Decentraland can purchase and sell digital real estate while exploring, engaging, and playing games in this virtual world. Users can now utilize interactive applications, peer-to-peer communication, and in-world payments thanks to the platform's growth.

Operations in Decentraland are regulated by two types of tokens.

These are:

• LAND — A non-fungible token used to define the ownership of digital real estate land parcels.

• MANA - A cryptocurrency that may be used to buy LAND and other virtual products and services in Decentraland.

Changes to the Decentraland software are made possible through a network of blockchain-based smart contacts that allow MANA owners to vote on land auctions, policy modifications, and new development subsidies.

Who is the creator of Decentraland?

Esteban Ordano and Ariel Meilich formed the Decentraland Foundation in 2015, responsible for developing the Decentraland software.

In 2017, the Decentraland team held an ICO to raise 86,206 ether (about $26 million at the time) to support its future operations. The Foundation, which owns 20% of the initial token supply, is also in charge of intellectual property and the Decentraland website.

Decentraland established a decentralized autonomous organization (DAO) to hand over project control to its users before releasing its platform. Furthermore, the original team claims to have deleted the private key that controlled Decentraland's smart contract.

How does Decentraland work?

The Decentraland program is used to keep track of real estate properties that are identified by the LAND token.

Users must retain their MANA token in an Ethereum wallet to participate with the program's ecosystem, which utilizes the Ethereum blockchain to track ownership of this digital land.

Developers can experiment with Decentraland's platform by customizing the animation and interactivity that users see on their virtual property.

The architecture of Decentraland is made up of many layered components that were constructed using Ethereum smart contracts.

A ledger in the consensus layer maintains track of land parcel ownership. Each LAND parcel has an owner, a virtual world coordinate, and a link to a description file that specifies the parcel's content.

The following files make up the content layer, which is in control of what happens within each parcel:

• Content Files - all static audio and visuals are referenced

• Interaction Definition – peer-to-peer interactions such as voice chat, gesturing, and messaging

• Script Files – describing the location and behavior of the referenced content

Finally, the real-time layer supports social interactions within Decentraland using user avatars and voice chat and messaging.

Marketplace and Builder

Users may also build settings outside of the game area with the help of a marketplace and a drag-and-drop editor built by the Decentraland team.

The marketplace allows users to manage and trade MANA-valued LAND tokens. The marketplace allows owners to purchase, sell, and trade parcels as well as other in-game items such as wearables and unique names.

It's worth mentioning that all transactions are settled between Ethereum wallets, and hence are confirmed and recorded on Ethereum's blockchain by the Ethereum network.

Decentraland's construction tools can be used by owners to create a unique experience inside their LAND parcels. Developers may use its editing tool to access customization libraries and payment implementations, allowing them to create interactive scenarios.

CHAPTER 15

HOW TO PURCHASE VIRTUAL LAND IN THE METAVERSE

A tract of virtual real estate represented by a non-fungible token is known as NFT metaverse land. The owner can use their property for gaming, socializing, work, advertising, and other uses depending on the platform.

You can purchase NFT metaverse land through a project's land sale or through an NFT marketplace where you can buy directly from landowners. To buy the land, you'll need a digital wallet and cryptocurrency. Land can also be sold to other users on various sites, and in the future, renting methods will be accessible.

Always purchase your NFT land from a project in a land sale or on the secondary market through a reputable NFT exchange. Make sure you comprehend the land's associated project and the financial risk you're taking on.

Tech lovers, investors, and crypto enthusiasts are becoming interested in the metaverse. Virtual land has become quite popular in the 3D digital world, and the market is very comparable to real-world real estate.

What is virtual NFT metaverse land?

NFT land is a buyable slice of digital space in a metaverse project. The owner of a Non-Fungible Token (NFT) can utilize the land for various purposes or pure speculation. A metaverse project's map is typically divided into smaller regions and sold as a single or numerous land offers. The most common method of payment is cryptocurrency; however, some projects also accept fiat.

When space is acquired, it usually comes with a 3D virtual experience for the owner and guests to enjoy. Because the lands are non-fungible tokens, proving ownership and validity of these digital assets is simple. The land owner can sell it on the secondary market or through the metaverse project ecosystem.

What are some of the applications of NFT virtual land?

While some investors may just be interested in making a profit, others may desire to use the land for its intended purpose. What you can accomplish with your land depends on the project you pick. If the land receives enough traffic, it is usual to hold events, conferences and even rent advertising space. Some businesses, such as PwC, have incorporated their land into their services. It's likely that if you buy land from an NFT game, you'll get in-game advantages from the plot.

How to purchase land in the metaverse

Acquiring NFT land is similar to purchasing any other NFT. To get started, all you need is a wallet and some cryptocurrency. Ensure you do your research before taking any risks, just like you would with any other investment.

Step 1: Choose a metaverse platform

You must first choose a metaverse platform before purchasing metaverse property. Your motives for purchasing the land will impact the project you choose. For this tutorial, we will use The Sandbox on Ethereum as an example,e but Decentraland is another popular alternative.

Step 2: Set up your wallet

You'll need to establish a wallet that allows you to access your cryptocurrency. Depending on your preferences, you can use a browser-based wallet or a mobile wallet. Using a browser-based wallet will usually result in fewer issues.

Both MetaMask and Binance Chain Wallet are good choices because they support different blockchains, but make sure the wallet you pick supports the NFT land blockchain.

You'll get a string of words known as your seed phrase when you set up your wallet. Keep it safe because this is how you will get your wallet back if you lose it. It's ideal for keeping it somewhere that's always offline.

124

Step 3: Link your wallet to the Sandbox marketplace

You can see plots of land available on The Sandbox's map. Some may be done directly through The Sandbox marketplace, while others must be done through third-party exchanges like OpenSea. To keep things simple, let's look at one we can bid on through The SandBox.

You must link your wallet before you can bid on anything. Click [Sign In] in the top right corner of The Sandbox map. In this example, make sure your wallet is set to the same blockchain as the project, Ethereum.

Next, click [MetaMask].

MetaMask will prompt you to connect in a pop-up window. Click [Next].

Click the [Connect] button to continue linking your wallet.

You will be prompted to enter an email address and a nickname in the Sandbox. To finish setting up your account, click [Continue]. If you want to use the SandBox editor, you can also freely provide a password.

Click [Sign] on the MetaMask signature request to finish your account.

You will see your profile picture and account balance in the upper right corner of the page once you've successfully connected.

You will see your profile picture and account balance in the upper right corner of the page once you've successfully connected.

Step 4: Go to Binance, buy SAND or ETH, and transfer it to your wallet.

You will need either Ether (ETH) or SAND in your wallet to buy or bid on land. Because most of The Sandbox land sales only accept ETH, purchasing ETH will likely be more beneficial. With your Binance account, you can buy SAND or ETH with a credit or debit card.

You will need to transfer your cryptocurrency to your crypto wallet once you've acquired it. Make a copy of your crypto wallet's public address and use it as your withdrawal address.

Step 5: Select a parcel of LAND

You can quickly sort through available land in The Sandbox to bid on or buy with the options below. Most of the Sandbox property has already been acquired; thus, you'll generally only discover land on OpenSea. You can still bid on these sales using The Sandbox map. Because OpenSea connections are incorporated in the UI, the SandBox map is also the best method to ensure that you've purchased a real NFT plot.

After you've found some land you wish to purchase, you can either put an offer by clicking the [Bid] button or purchase it for a fixed price by clicking the ETH amount. Let's look at how to make a bid by clicking [Bid].

A pop-up window will appear, allowing you to make an offer. Before finalizing the transaction with your wallet, enter the bid amount and click [Place Bid]. If the sale ends or the seller rejects your bid, the cryptocurrency will be refunded to your wallet.

If you click on the fixed price, you will be transported to OpenSea to complete the purchase. Before buying the land, you'll need to link your wallet to the marketplace. If you don't want to use The Sandbox, you can offer through OpenSea.

How to sell land in the metaverse

When selling your NFT Land, you typically have two options. You can sell it on the metaverse project's marketplace or a secondary market. Only third-party marketplaces can presently be used for sales in The Sandbox. Landowners will be able to sell directly through The Sandbox in the future for a 5 percent transaction fee in SAND.

Go to your profile, then click the [Sell] button on your NFT to sell your land on OpenSea. You'll be able to set a fixed price or a timed auction after that.

How to rent land in the metaverse

Landowners will rent their land to other parties in some projects, such as The Sandbox. There is, however, no official framework in place to accomplish this. If you decide to rent your land to someone, you'll have to make a private agreement, making the procedure rather risky. When renting, you should never give the renter ownership of your NFT. It's safer to wait until an official secure rental scheme is launched.

Tips before buying NFT virtual land

When investing in NFT land, you should always follow the best procedures, like with any other investment. You purchase NFT land, be sure to utilize the official project link or a reliable third-party marketplace. Before you purchase, do some research on the platform you're interested in and make sure you understand its basics. Remember that purchasing property isn't your only option; you might be able to rent land in the future if you need it for a certain reason.

The digital real estate ecosystem has exploded in popularity in the cryptocurrency realm. As you can see, purchasing and selling land is pretty simple. On the other hand, current pricing might make it more expensive than a physical real estate investment. If you decide to buy NFT metaverse land, ensure you consider the risks and stick to safe crypto activities.

CHAPTER 16

DECENTRALIZED FINANCE (DEFI)

Cryptocurrencies have grown into a trillion-dollar business, causing a wave of financial upheaval throughout the globe.

Cryptocurrencies have a long history. The invention dates back to the 1980s, when cryptography improvements were made. Since then, a succession of events has impacted the crypto world, the most notable of which is the first cryptocurrency, Bitcoin. Despite its meteoric rise over the last twelve years, financial services for Bitcoin have been slow to emerge, owing to its fundamental lack of stability and acceptance. Because of its price fluctuation, mainstream banks will not accept a Bitcoin loan, making Bitcoin a poor asset for correctly planning any investment.

Things move rapidly in the crypto world, and DeFi is a hot topic right now - it's an exciting space to be. If you're still clueless, let's go a bit more into DeFi and discover more about it.

Decentralized finance, or DeFi, is an umbrella word for many public blockchain applications and initiatives aimed at challenging the existing banking industry. Inspired by blockchain technology, decentralized finance is referred to as financial applications based on blockchain technologies, generally employing smart contracts. Smart contracts are enforceable agreements that are automated and accessible by anyone with an internet connection. They do not need any middlemen to execute and can access anyone with an internet connection.

DeFi refers to apps and peer-to-peer protocols built on decentralized blockchain networks that allow for simple borrowing, lending, and trading of financial instruments without requiring access rights. The Ethereum network is used in most DeFi applications today, but many more public networks are emerging that provide better speed, security, scalability, and lower costs.

Why smart contracts?

Most smart contracts include Turing Complete programming languages, which enable numerous parties to communicate without the need for a centralized middleman. The ability of blockchain to make use of smart contracts has made it an attractive platform for developing financial applications.

What was the origin of DeFi?

Initially, humans bartered for commodities and services. However, as humans evolved, so did economies: we established money to make it simpler to trade commodities and services. As a result, coins aided in introducing new technologies and improved economic levels. Progress comes at a cost.

Central authorities have traditionally issued currencies that underlie our economy, which has given them greater influence as more people have come to trust them. However, on occasion, trust has been breached, leading to concerns about the centralized authority's capacity to handle the money. DeFi was created to build an open financial system that removes the need to trust and depend on a central authority.

DeFi, according to some, began in 2009 with the debut of Bitcoin, the first peer-to-peer digital currency built on top of the blockchain network. The notion of introducing revolution into the conventional financial sector through blockchains became a necessary next step in decentralising legacy financial institutions thanks to Bitcoin. All of this was made possible with the development of Ethereum and, more especially, smart contracts in 2015. The Ethereum network is a second-generation blockchain that was the first to use the technology's promise in the financial sector fully. It incentivizes firms and organizations to develop and deploy projects that make up the DeFi ecosystem.

DeFi provided many opportunities for creating a transparent and robust financial system that is not controlled by a single entity. However, 2017 saw the beginning of a new era for financial apps, with initiatives allowing for more than simply money transfers.

Challenges within centralized finance

Financial markets can empower innovative ideas and create societal prosperity. Even still, these marketplaces have a concentrated power structure. People who invest in the current financial system hand over their assets to intermediaries like banks and financial institutions, which keeps risk and control at the forefront of these systems.

Bankers and institutions have a history of failing to identify market risks, as seen by the 2008 financial crisis. Without a doubt, when central authorities manage money, risk builds up in the centre, endangering the whole system.

Bitcoin and other early cryptocurrencies were merely decentralized in terms of issuance and storage, despite being designed to allow people total control over their assets. Until the advent of smart contracts, which allowed DeFi, providing access to a larger variety of financial instruments remained a challenge.

DeFi protocols and how they work

DeFi has evolved into a whole ecosystem of functional apps and standards that benefit millions. DeFi ecosystems currently hold over $30 billion in assets, making it one of the fastest-growing segments of the public blockchain space.

Here's a rundown of the most common DeFi use cases and protocols on the market right now:

DeFi lending and borrowing

DeFi gave finance a new path by allowing lending and borrowing. Crypto investors might receive annual returns on their investments thanks to decentralized funding, often known as 'Open Finance.' Individuals might borrow money at a set interest rate thanks to decentralized borrowing. The goal of borrowing and lending is to meet the demands of the bitcoin community while also serving financial sector use cases.

Compound Finance is a leading DeFi lending and borrowing platform.

Rober Leshner came up with the idea for Compound Finance, which he launched in 2018. The project is an Ethereum-based lending system that enables users to earn interest by lending out assets or taking out loans against collateral. This is made possible via the Compound protocol, which uses computer algorithms to calculate interest rates to provide liquidity for cryptocurrencies.

How does Compound work?

Users of Compound earn interest by depositing cryptocurrency. The following is a list of the cryptocurrencies that may be deposited on the protocol and the predicted Annual Percentage Yield (APY). Users can utilize cryptocurrencies as collateral for loans once they are available on the Compound platform.

Compound token: $COMP

The Compound protocol governance token, $COMP, is a token that allows its holders to recommend and execute development modifications to the protocol. The following changes have been made:

Choosing which digital assets to support.

Modifications to the distribution of $COMP tokens.

Adapting the platform's collateralization criteria.

Decentralized exchanges

Decentralized Exchanges (DEx) are one of DeFi's most important features, as they lock the most capital compared to other DeFi protocols. DExs let users trade tokens for other assets without needing a centralized intermediary or custodian. Traditional exchanges (centralized exchanges) provide comparable services, but the investments available are subject to the will and expenses of the exchange. Another disadvantage of CExs is the additional cost of each transaction, addressed with DExs.

What are the primary benefits of DeFi?

Traditional finance depends on banks and courts to function as middlemen and arbitrators.

There are no intermediaries or arbitrators required in DeFi applications. The code outlines how any potential disagreement will be resolved, and users retain complete control over their funds at all times. This lowers the costs of offering and utilizing these products and makes the financial system more frictionless.

Single points of failure are removed because these new financial services are built on top of blockchains. The data is stored on the blockchain and distributed across hundreds of nodes, making censorship or a service challenge possible closure.

Deploying a DeFi application becomes significantly less complex and safe since frameworks for DeFi apps can be built in advance.

Another key benefit of such an open ecosystem is the simplicity with which those who would otherwise be unable to obtain financial services can do so. Since the conventional financial system depends on intermediaries generating a profit, its services are often unavailable in low-income areas. However, with DeFi, the fees are substantially lower, and low-income people can use a wider choice of financial services.

What are some of the possible applications for DeFi?

Lending & Borrowing

One of the most popular applications in the DeFi ecosystem is open lending protocols. The benefits of open, decentralized borrowing and lending over the conventional credit system are many. These include no credit checks, the ability to collateralize digital assets, instant transaction settlement, and the possibility of future standardization are among them.

Since these loan services are based on public blockchains, they need less trust and are protected by cryptographic verification mechanisms. Blockchain-based loan platforms decrease counterparty risk, making borrowing and lending more affordable, quicker, and accessible to a wider range of individuals.

Monetary banking services

Financial banking services are a clear use case for DeFi apps since they are, by definition, financial applications. These can include the issuance of stablecoins, insurance, and mortgages.

The creation of stablecoins is becoming more important as the blockchain industry matures. They are a crypto asset that is generally linked to a physical asset but can be easily moved digitally. Decentralized stablecoins could be accepted daily as digital cash that is neither issued nor managed by a central body, given that cryptocurrency values can change fast at times.

The process of obtaining a mortgage is costly and time-consuming, owing to the many intermediaries that must be engaged. Underwriting and legal expenses might be greatly lowered if smart contracts are used.

Insurance on the blockchain could remove the need for intermediaries and enable risk to be distributed among many people. This might lead to reduced premiums while maintaining the same level of service.

Decentralized Marketplaces

This category of applications can be difficult to evaluate because it is the part of DeFi that provides for the greatest financial innovation.

Decentralized exchanges are perhaps some of the most important DeFi applications (DEXes). These platforms enable users to trade digital assets without requiring their funds to be held by a trusted intermediary (an exchange). With smart contracts, transactions are done directly between user wallets.

Decentralized exchanges often offer cheaper trading costs than centralized exchanges since they require less maintenance.

A wide range of traditional financial products may also be issued and owned using blockchain technology. These apps would operate decentralised, eliminating the need for custodians and single points of failure.

For example, security token issuance platforms may offer issuers the tools and resources they need to launch tokenized securities on the blockchain with their own set of specifications.

Other efforts might lead to derivatives, decentralized prediction markets, synthetic assets, and more.

CHAPTER 17

BEST METAVERSE CRYPTO TO INVEST IN 2022

The metaverse is a virtual extension of our actual existence. From anywhere globally, you can spend time with friends and relatives there, socializing at concerts or art galleries. And, given the platform's digital structure, it's only natural that cryptos would coexist with the metaverse. It is already being used to purchase land and items from online retailers within virtual worlds. Metaverse cryptos are, unsurprisingly, all the rage right now. And as the notion grows in popularity, so will these coins.

Because cryptocurrencies are highly volatile investments, it's critical to understand the risks before investing in any funds. Even if speculators appear to have driven a coin higher, hidden risks may make it less secure for normal investors. This is incredibly risky for individuals who don't keep up with tech news or have a limited budget, as they may miss out on other options (like stocks.)

Before, social networking platforms like Microsoft's (NASDAQ: MSFT), Meta's (NASDAQ: FB), Facebook, or Linkedin were multibillion-dollar businesses; they were preceded by other sites that were less successful. This serves as a reminder not to dismiss the metaverse if it first fails to catch on; instead, we should keep an eye out for new applications with potential. As a result, coins and tokens that deal with this new investing field are worthy of your attention.

If you wish to participate in this popular movement, here are five metaverse cryptos to consider:

Decentraland (CCC: MANA-USD)

Ethereum (CCC: ETH-USD)

The Sandbox (CCC: SAND-USD)

Enjin Coin (CCC:ENJ-USD)

Axie Infinity (CCC: AXS-USD)

Decentraland (MANA)

VR is the next big thing in gaming, and you can get a taste of it right now with Decentraland. You don't need any cryptocurrency or headgear to explore this virtual environment.

There are different ways to play the game, including purchasing and developing a virtual plot of land. You can use mazes and casinos to help you navigate this digital world that others have constructed for you.

In 2017, the Decentraland project was founded to create an immersive virtual environment on the blockchain. It has had a lot of time to flourish since then, all because this digital world is similar to, but also separate from, our reality.

Users can take a break from their daily routines by strolling across town or visiting an interactive art gallery. There's also much for gamers in this online space, with immersive experiences available right at your computer desk.

Last year, Decentraland presented the world's first multi-day music event. The festival brought together more than 80 musicians from across the world, including Paris Hilton and electronic dance music legend Deadmau5.

Decentraland fared extremely well last year due to its first-mover advantage, rising from under a dollar to almost $5.50 in November. Since then, the token has lost a lot of traction. However, as

Decentraland grows in value and popularity, investing in it is wise. MANA remains one of the greatest metaverse cryptos available, despite its being still in its early stages.

The Sandbox (SAND)

In the same way that Decentraland enables you to acquire land, develop games, and share them with others, the Sandbox lets you do the same. Although the two projects are highly competitive, they have a similar aesthetic.

Both were founded around the same period and share a lot of principles. There are significant contrasts, though; for example, The Sandbox hasn't yet revealed its whole virtual environment to all players, making it rather exclusive for the time being.

The Sandbox, on the other hand, is the greatest place to start with non-fungible tokens (NFTs). It enables more personalization and a greater emphasis on producing unique goods that gamers can buy or sell for coins.

Users may create their games, which they can then play or exchange with other players on the platform's partner websites. Several notable personalities and franchises, such as Snoop Dogg and The Walking Dead, are among them.

It was just a matter of time until The Sandbox's metaverse achieved the same level of popularity. The project has been in development since 2011. However, like Decentraland, it exploded in popularity at the end of last year. SoftBank (OTCMKTS: SFTBY) backed it up with a $93 million investment to help it get its product to market faster.

Currently, the cryptocurrency market is in the red. However, there are ways for investors to profit. One such potential is The Sandbox's new Mega City initiative, which allows users to purchase virtual land and sell it as soon as they're ready. If done correctly, it can provide big — and rapid — profits to investors.

When judging metaverse cryptos, The Sandbox and Decentraland may appear to be interchangeable. However, certain major distinctions meet the diverse needs investing requirements. As a result, you must invest accordingly.

Ethereum (ETH)

Ethereum has been around since 2015 and is one of the most popular coins on our list. It's also open-source crypto that runs its internal processes and decentralized apps using blockchain technology (dApps). This implies that other parties, such as banks, will no longer profit from transactions.

Even though there are so many different cryptocurrencies out there right now, one of the best things about Ethereum is how steady its value can be. Because they are founded on similar ideas, these options may change often. Nonetheless, each has something special to offer investors.

The Ethereum network is the world's most active blockchain, making it a natural choice for metaverse developers. Almost every cryptocurrency on this list follows ERC-20 specifications and runs its projects on this reliable platform.

Ethereum is a popular cryptocurrency for buying metaverse real estate. The NFT boom, which continues to take place on this network, employs ETH as its primary currency.

It's also worth mentioning that Ethereum will switch from a proof-of-work consensus system to proof-of-stake mining this year. As a result, ETH appears to be a good crypto investment this year.

Axie Infinity (AXS)

Investors have been keeping an eye on Axie Infinity for quite some time. Many people think of it as a video game investment, but they're starting to understand the possibilities of spending their money on virtual real estate instead.

The Axie Infinity world grew to fame in just one summer. This was first seen in July when their AXS token skyrocketed. That was when the metaverse notion started gaining traction and popularity.

So far this year, Axie Infinity has witnessed massive growth. Cute (and un) Axies ariquee inspired by the top-performing coin. Players can breed or raise them to compete for victory against other breeders and breeds on the marketplace. Furthermore, you can sell them.

Axie is a unique game in which participants are rewarded with bitcoin outside of the app. This concept has piqued people's interest, particularly during Covid-19. Many people were seeking methods to supplement their income beyond their paychecks and savings accounts. Axie's play-to-earn strategy allows you to advance through levels and earn cryptocurrency.

In an increasingly digital society, Axie Infinity allows users to invest in real estate through tokenized pieces of land. You will be able to buy and develop these properties yourself, but there will also be alternative options to sell your ownership in the near future.

Enjin Coin (ENJ)

Enjin is making investing in the metaverse easier than ever before. This platform will be a powerhouse in the virtual property sector for years to come, with new partnerships and initiatives debuting every day. While Enjin does not yet have its metaverse, it does provide easy ways to create tokenized assets.

Enjin is a blockchain platform that can be used to power various games. These NFTs can be purchased or earned and stored in players' safe wallets on the network's dedicated domain. Alternatively, developers can adapt them to various platforms if necessary.

Many gamers have wished for a means to own and manage their digital assets across many games for the past decade. They've finally found it with Enjin. This platform allows you to create your own NFTs, which you can then spend in any game that accepts them or sell on the network's marketplace.

The growing blockchain gaming network also focuses on virtual real estate beyond tokenized commodities. The program, which lets users purchase a piece of real estate using their preferred cryptocurrency, isn't only for investors. It has far-reaching implications for today's society and the future economy.

CHAPTER 18

HOW TO INVEST AND PROFIT FROM

METAVERSE

For a long time, virtual spaces and worlds have been popular. People became immersed in virtual environments through games like Sims City and the GTA series. Virtual worlds, also known as 'MetaVerse,' have been a successful addition to future technology due to these games becoming a worldwide sensation.

Over time, metaverses have advanced to the point that people have begun to see this technology as economically advantageous to the world. Metaverses were virtual tools with no reality-based reference before incorporating this worldview.

Another area that has significantly impacted the market's general circumstances is cryptocurrency and blockchain. The market has been presented with actual and industrial-based solutions due to the widespread use of blockchain. Digital-based technology is expected to take over the role of offering monetary-based solutions to the rest of the globe.

Metaverse, as a phenomenon, is founded on science fiction. It is made up of 2 prefixes: "meta" for "beyond" and "verse" for "universe." The Metaverse is the ultimate result of all the internet-enabled virtual worlds that have been built. Virtual reality and augmented reality have successfully created avatars that communicate virtually and have digital assets that are end-to-end blockchain encrypted. It is a virtual-reality environment where people interact with one another in an auto-generated setting.

Metaverses have been around for a while, but the underlying technology has yet to bring permissionless identities, financial services, or high-speed exchanges to the general market. To create a reality-based connection between the virtual and real worlds, cryptocurrencies and blockchain developed a system for sharing and saving the data of billions of people.

As Metaverses became more focused on using blockchain technology as an 'engine' for these platforms, metaverses' whole concept of operation changed dramatically. Because metaverses are virtual worlds, they have always had a financial system. Before blockchain became a part of the virtual world, these in-game currencies had no value because they lacked a physical form. The concept of 'Decentralization' affected the platforms soon after blockchain was integrated into the Metaverse phenomena. Platforms based on blockchain technology had their own NFTs and cryptocurrency, which were used to create, own, and monetize virtual assets. One of the technology's breakthroughs The genuine worth that might be established by permitting selling NFTs into real cash through the Metaverse's specialized NFT marketplaces was. Axie Infinity, Decentraland, and SecondLive are examples of virtual worlds that have become commercial sensations, allowing people to make a fortune by being a part of them.

How to Invest in MetaVerses?

People were introduced to various types of entries as metaverses normalized as a system that runs over the blockchain. Investors can invest in both active and passive ways in the virtual world, depending on how it runs.

The user was actively interested in playing the game and participating in the virtual world. As a full universe, Metaverses had a plethora of categories, each with its own set of applications. A player that plays in the game and is a part of the Metaverse earns money and NFT tokens (that the Metaverse runs on). These gained tokens are valuable in the financial world and can be traded on any metaverse's markets. Furthermore, users have the option of exchanging tokens for major cryptocurrencies.

Users are permitted to invest passively in the Metaverse while focusing on the active investing style. The NFT token, which is utilized across the Metaverse, or NFT Metaverse, has a monetary value in the crypto world. As the project grows, it can list itself on various exchanges and platforms. Investors can pool their money across the exchange or platform to earn profits because it is a part of several IDOs and launchpads. This brings us to the end of investors' passive participation in the Metaverse.

Another approach to investing in Metaverses that might be recognized is investors' exposure by purchasing a Metaverse ETF. An exchange-traded fund (ETF) is a collection of securities and safeties that trade like stocks on a stock market. Investors can invest in companies that already have a strong foothold in the crypto ecosystem through a metaverse stock ETF.

How to Profit from MetaVerse?

Being a part of the game is one of the most understandable explanations offered to the user on making money in the Metaverse. Because these metaverses use the 'Play-to-Earn' mechanism, you can earn a significant amount of money just by playing the game.

Another way for profiting from metaverses is through passive investing. People are urged to do their research on a project before investing. Discovering the project's outstanding use cases and road plan is something that can provide you with extreme benefits in a short length of time.

The Metaverse is growing tenfold as a technology. There is a lot to present because these systems are boundless to perform a wide range of operations across the virtual world. As we all agree that the scope of metaverses is infinite, many use cases can be implemented. If you want to profit from the metaverse, you need to develop your conceptual understanding. This will ultimately lead to more concepts and distinctiveness in metaverses. Investing in technology on your own would help you make it incredibly profitable.

Virtual worlds and the Metaverse have offered a logical strategy for linking the digital and physical worlds. Blockchain was one of the most notable factors that arrived to branch the connection definitively. Metaverse provides users with a variety of options and the ability to profit excessively from the system.

CHAPTER 19

MISCONCEPTIONS ABOUT METAVERSE

The concept of Metaverse — an alternate world enabled by advanced technology — is recognizable through entertainment, films, and literature, although sounding difficult to fathom when applied to our daily life.

You might see "Ready Player One," in which the entire world is hooked to playing the same VR game; "Altered Carbon," in which your consciousness can be downloaded into a new body; and, of course, the "Matrix." The dystopian aspect that exposes the dark truth and future of humans exploring alternative realms is a recurrent theme in these (and other) novels and movies.

Even though we like these films, there is a lot more to the Metaverse concept and the benefits (yes, there are many!) it offers in our daily lives. We will debunk some of the common myths regarding this occurrence in this section.

It is not one world — it is multiple worlds!

The term "metaverse" does not indicate a single alternate world developed by a large technology company with the objective of controlling every element of people's lives. On the contrary, a comprehensive collection of technologies like 3D graphics, VR, MR, AI, and blockchain that connect it to the real-world economy allows anybody to construct their universe, complete with its own set of laws and possibilities. Decentraland, Cryptovoxels, The Sandbox, and Somnium Space are the four primary Metaverses discussed nowadays by specialists (VR-backed reality).

Alternative realities defined by complex settings, meaningful game history, and well-designed characters are created by innovative teams of developers from both well-known and obscure gaming studios. It's totally up to you to decide which universe you wish to be a part of (if any at all!).

Metaverse is not a Facebook invention.

To expand on the preceding argument, it's important to note that Metaverse was neither established nor managed by Facebook. True, most people first heard of this phrase when Mark Zuckerberg announced Facebook's renaming to "Meta" in October 2021, but he was only following a trend gaining traction for some years.

According to myth, Neal Stephenson, a science fiction writer, created the term "metaverse" when he released his novel "Snow Crash" in 1992.

A speech with magical force.

These days, people don't believe in such things. Unless you're in the Metaverse, where magic is conceivable. The Metaverse is a code-based fictional system. And code is simply a type of communication that computers can understand. According to Neal Stephenson, the whole

Metaverse may be viewed as an one massive nam-shub, implementing itself on L. Bob Rife's fiber-optic network.

To cut a long story short, while we may expect some important projects and advancements in this sector from Facebook, the Metaverse will never be controlled or defined by the company.

It's not just about gaming

Gaming is the first use of alternate worlds and affects many people. With its events, Metaverse has evolved into a major stage for the entertainment sector. Decentraland tries to create a unique musical experience for its thousands of virtual spectators by hosting a four-day Metaverse Festival with headliners DEADMAU5, Paris Hilton, and 3LAU.

However, something big is happening right before our eyes as millions of people play their favorite games: play-to-earn gaming communities are practicing true democracy and freedom of expression and governance through decentralized autonomous organizations (DAOs). Everyone can take control of a project's future development as a major decision-maker by using governance tokens. Imagine the impact this technology can have when applied to our everyday lives after it has been perfected in the game industry!

Meanwhile, gaming guilds, which bring together thousands of gamers, will have the opportunity to create the economy they want while considering their members' needs. Guilds examine all of the developer's suggestions and recommend the best course of action for meeting the majority's needs.

It's made to help you create money rather than deplete your bank account.

It's simple to picture blowing all of your money on virtual items in a virtual environment. You can make a living in the Metaverse, as in reality. Jobs that didn't exist before are being created by the new reality, and it's time to try out for something new. Personal advisers in the fields of NFT assets or art, for example, may make a fortune by staying on top of the newest trends. You never know what hard talents may be required for Metaverse reality – an avatar stylist, for example, may find work if a player needs to personalize his appearance. You didn't come up with the idea to give the gorilla's avatar such a lovely headgear, did you?

You can earn tokens that can be traded for crypto or fiat by winning leaderboards and tournaments in the game. Play-to-earn is an entirely new market idea coined by Metaverse. Metaguild and other gaming guilds provide the ability to begin earning money with no initial investment or knowledge.

Metaverse is either a bad or dangerous

However, there are also concerns about Metaverse's vulnerability as a target for hackers. Although the alternate world provides us with limitless potential, it also poses tremendous risks for stolen valuables. Furthermore, a worldwide power grid issue has become crucial in terms of blockchain technology use.

Returning to science fiction's famous dystopian cliches, we hope that the various points we made in this section were sufficient to convince you — or at least to start the conversation! — The Metaverse is something we co-create to have a beneficial influence on the lives of millions of people.

CONCLUSION

The metaverse as a whole is a fairly futuristic concept with several advantages. With the introduction of metaverse technology, virtual living standards will increase, and digital platforms will be merged into a single section.

The metaverse is the internet's next generation.

It's centred on things you can do with your friends and colleagues.

Creation's exponential growth is mixing-and-matching, embedding, and connecting, using a new age of creator-oriented technologies.

Medical experts can now treat easily detectable diseases at an early stage thanks to metaverse technology. Thanks to this technology, customers will be able to see things displayed by retail merchants.

The game world, which will seem more genuine thanks to a metaverse, will be the most diverse use of this technology. Additionally, this technology will improve the travel experience by enabling users to go to distant locations through a metaverse. Aside from these, several more advantages will become apparent over time.

It'll transport you to places you never imagined.

And it is awesome.

Made in the USA
Las Vegas, NV
06 May 2022